'Rachel Ellison is pioneering in relation to coaching been highly valued in the field of psychotherapy – de sonal way, complete with rich details and intricacies reader can follow the narrative of each case through the eyes of both the client and the coach, with additional insights provided by the psychoanalytically oriented supervision group. The stories offer a deep questioning of the "good practice" imperatives of the field and challenge many traditional interpretations of how the coaching process should proceed. It is not a book with "how to" strategies for being a coach or a coaching client. It offers something much more important – a glimpse into the real struggles and delights of the coaching encounter.'

Tatiana Bachkirova, Professor of Coaching Psychology and Director of the International Centre for Coaching and Mentoring Studies at Oxford Brookes University

'From her position of trust coaching leaders in some of the most challenging situations and her own personal experience, Rachel Ellison offers a wealth of insight which is relevant to leaders in all walks of life. Her observations of the psychological importance of space and environment in a neonatal intensive care unit, mirror some of the challenges faced by businesses seeking to reconcile the spiraling costs of city-based property and a desire felt by many employees to work more flexibly outside the office. In the supermarket chapter, we meet a World Foods buyer who is truly trying to embrace and harness the power of diversity (a word too often used to refer only to matters of gender or race) to create commercial as well as cultural successes, experiences that can be applied by us all. Packed with reflective learning, this is a book I keep going back to and every time I do, I find something new to think about.'

Jenny Hearn, Director PWC

'Rachel Ellison's book speaks to everyone who has leadership responsibilities and teams to manage. Her meticulously researched case studies shed light on the issues leaders face across a fascinating range of organisations and cultures. By focusing on individuals and how they respond to very specific personal challenges in settings from prison to Paralympics, Rachel draws lessons which apply across large and small organisations. She shows how leaders grow through awareness of their own background and motives; and how important it is to engage honestly with others, respecting their culture and outlook. This book will be invaluable for everyone who wants to connect with those they lead, and to understand what real leadership means in a global context.'

Sir Martin Donnelly, KCB, CMG, former Permanent Secretary for the Department for International Trade and the Department for Business Innovation and Skills

'In the well-populated field of leadership coaching books this one is different. It demonstrates how leadership takes many different guises but the qualities it requires are the same and the questions a Coach needs to explore are as relevant in times of cultural change as in active conflict zones as in board rooms. This thought provoking account of the writer's experiences provides insights about how a Coach can enable the navigation of different leadership situations by considering the hidden story as well as the presenting facts. And a bonus for the reader is the stimulus questions at the end of each chapter – particularly valuable for Coach Supervision groups!'

Liz Macann, former Head of Coaching, BBC

'Diversity is key to this engaging discussion of what leadership means. Ellison has a unique ability to plot psychological learning against a backdrop of real human theatre. The canvas moves from Afghanistan to Jerusalem, from cycling to salami, from the authenticity of leadership to the authenticity of gherkins. The world has needed someone to come out and say authoritatively that diversity will help your organisation thrive more successfully and do your job better. What Ellison is telling us is that diversity is not a tick box exercise but a vital tool and in fact a requirement of effective leadership. Ellison says you win trust by learning and listening, and she doesn't shrink from the big questions, such as what leadership teaches us about ourselves and about those around us?

I loved this book and the idea that leaders are leaders, all over the world and in every walk of life. Buy a copy of this book if you want to learn about diversity of teams, how women are empowered when they join together and how commercial success and collaboration in business can be a shared cow.'

Rebecca Hilsenrath, Chief Executive,
Equality and Human Rights Commission

'Rachel's deep and diverse insights are brilliantly brought to life through a number of fascinating case studies in this valuable contribution to the literature of leadership. Covering an extremely broad spectrum, from the deeply personal account of the experiences inside a neonatal intensive care unit, to the powerful story of NGO leadership in a war zone, Rachel shows that whilst the situations may differ the fundamental challenges of leadership are universal. This book is a great resource for anyone wanting to explore leadership: accessibly written, thought-provoking and universally applicable.'

Andrew Hodgson, Head of Finance Northern Europe, Uber

'I often find it difficult to find a business book that stimulates my thinking and emotions. Rachel Ellison's book clearly does this. I felt a personal connection and empathy with the leaders sharing their stories and could relate to the challenges they face. The real-life, non-corporate situations create powerful perspectives that are thought provoking and inspirational. It is a reminder to business leaders, sports coaches and parents of their responsibilities to care for their teams and families, as a collective of individuals with their own needs and to be a catalyst for each person to achieve their aspirations. The book challenges traditional ways of thinking with humility and in a non-arrogant style.'

Geoff Ranson, Senior Director, Internal Audit Asda Wal-Mart

'This highly accessible book challenges us in an understanding of leadership that extends far beyond the more commonly defined competencies of envisioning the future and inspiring followers. It invites us to explore the critical effect of the emotional labour of work on the individual, the group and the organisation. Through the range of evocative narratives, we are invited to tolerate, feel and think about deeper, usually covert, dynamics of organisational life. The book offers a gift of insight to leaders.'

Wendy Harding, PhD, CEO and Director of Academic Programs, National Institute of Organisation Dynamics, Australia

'Every day leaders in all fields wrestle with stressful situations, but not many of us work in war zones or face life and death situations. This book draws vivid lessons from the experience of those courageous people who do. It analyses different responses to acute stress. It points the way to positive, life-enhancing solutions to extreme demands. I recommend the stories Rachel Ellison tells so well to anyone looking for inspiration for their own leadership role.'

Alan Bookbinder, former Director, Sainsbury Family Charitable Trusts

'This book presents us with diverse and deeply personal stories. It challenges us to embed the powerful lessons within them into our professional lives. As an educator, the text encouraged me to find vital learning about our work environment, space and boundaries, even from the most extreme and distressing circumstances. I was engrossed by the leader's stories but really appreciated how the author summarised each chapter by directing the reader to reflect on their own thinking and learning. Ellison's insight, pace and clarity makes for a thought provoking read with lasting impact.'

Niki Jackson, Director of Education NNLS/Youth Education Director

'Rachel draws on the varied and fascinating experiences that coaching has exposed her to, creating a book that is colourful, thought-provoking and hard to put down. I especially liked the story of Fatima in Somalia and the near-impossible leadership choices she has to make. Rachel's analysis goes beyond the obvious and looks at upbringing, culture and personal drivers to help both leaders and coaches untangle complex issues at work. I loved it. Deeply enjoyable.'

Anthony Ryland, former Learning & Development Director, Samsung Electronics

'We lead in a very different world today where so many rules are being rewritten in all organisations – private, public, NGO. Coaching is one essential tool which will allow us to lead effectively in such a changed world. Rachel Ellison's fresh and provocative book challenges us in powerful ways as to how as leaders and coaches we must raise our game to remain relevant and excellent in this new world.'

Alan Smith, Senior Executive at a global financial services organisation

'This fascinating, insightful book takes the reader on a journey of others' leadership experiences and coaching challenges, from the hot, dangerous war zones of Afghanistan and Syria to the mosaic tiled floors of the National Gallery, London. In each of its chapters, the author skillfully blends a personal human story with deeper more psychoanalytical insights, which can only leave us thinking harder about our leadership and interactions with colleagues. Equally skillfully the book draws out reflections for both leaders and coaches, the two complementary perspectives making it a particularly useful tool for each.'

Tim Stew, British High Commissioner to Trinidad & Tobago, Foreign & Commonwealth Office

'Rachel thoughtfully examines the essential importance of investing time in relationship building with your suppliers, and of really getting to know your team and nurture it. The international supermarket chapter skillfully raises questions about FMCG food retail in 21st century Britain, the deeper meaning and role of food in the lives of communities around the world, the type of food we buy and why. If only most consumers had the chance to read this chapter and build an understanding of the unique supply chains giving them access to wonderful produce. A must read for leaders, coaches and consumers.'

Jane Steward, Managing Director, Eastgate Larder

'This book provides a fascinating insight into both the art and the science of leadership coaching. The case studies are compelling and (sometimes uncomfortably) honest. The insight into how a coach picks up on signals, chooses what to name and how to frame questions will make me more self-aware as well as more observant of the unspoken, and perhaps even subconscious, queues from those who work with and for me. This book can help on the journey to becoming a transformational and not just a transactional leader.'

Emma Squire, Director of Arts, Heritage and Tourism, Department for Digital, Culture, Media & Sport

'Rachel Ellison's book about leadership and coaching is incomparably fresh. Instead of shop worn theories of coaching pummeled by tired ideas, we are brought into the life space of her clients as they live and breathe their leadership challenges and dilemmas. From a refugee camp to neonatal intensive care, to elite high-performance para sport, this is a book about leadership as it is lived in the raw and about a coach who meets her clients where their experience, intellect and emotions converge. You the reader are invited to inhabit Ellison's world and to learn along with her what it is like to help leaders achieve programmatic and moral excellence.'

Dr Larry Hirschhorn, Director, Centre for Applied Research, Philadelphia, USA; Chair Bridger Memorial Award Committee, ISPSO

Global Leadership & Coaching

Global Leadership & Coaching: Flourishing Under Intense Pressure at Work is a unique and personal look at coaching, leading and working internationally, bringing together inspiring, original and dramatic stories of leadership from around the world. From war zones to refugee camps, prisons to hospitals, elite sport to supermarkets, each case study draws on psychoanalytic below-the-surface thinking to analyse, interpret and understand a leaders' decisions, motivations and fears.

Rachel Ellison's inter-cultural approach takes us to Afghanistan, Syria and Iraq, Sudan, Somalia and the Central African Republic, to Honduras, the Czech Republic, the USA and the UK. *Global Leadership & Coaching* presents a series of individual case studies from Ellison's own experiences working with senior commercial, public and third sector leaders across 35 different countries, cultures and organisational contexts. Compellingly written, this book explores a diverse range of themes to consider when managing risk, danger and extreme emotional stress in some of the most hazardous and challenging work environments. Throughout the text, leaders share their stories of learning how to lead and develop others.

Accessible, engaging and original research, *Global Leadership & Coaching: Flourishing Under Intense Pressure at Work* is essential reading for today's leaders and aspiring leaders looking to develop themselves personally and professionally. This book is also a resource for coaches and coach supervisors. *Global Leadership & Coaching* provides contemporary, practical and applicable examples of excellence in leadership, for individuals and organisations seeking to develop a high performance, reflective and reflexive corporate learning culture, which enables employees to successfully navigate challenge, increase productivity and find joy in coming to work.

Rachel Ellison, MBE, is a former BBC news correspondent and international development aid programme director. She is now an executive leadership coach based in London, UK.

Global Leadership & Coaching

Flourishing Under Intense Pressure at Work

Rachel Ellison

Routledge
Taylor & Francis Group
LONDON AND NEW YORK

First published 2019
by Routledge
2 Park Square, Milton Park, Abingdon, Oxon OX14 4RN

and by Routledge
52 Vanderbilt Avenue, New York, NY 10017

Routledge is an imprint of the Taylor & Francis Group, an informa business

British Library Cataloguing-in-Publication Data
A catalogue record for this book is available from the British Library

Library of Congress Cataloging-in-Publication Data
Names: Ellison, Rachel, author.
Title: Global leadership and coaching : flourishing under intense pressure at work / Rachel Ellison.
Description: Abingdon, Oxon ; New York, NY : Routledge, 2019. | Includes index.
Identifiers: LCCN 2018034965 (print) | LCCN 2018037811 (ebook) | ISBN 9781351346207 (Abode Reader) | ISBN 9781351346191 (Epub) | ISBN 9781351346184 (Mobipocket) | ISBN 9781138564947 (hardback) | ISBN 9781138564961 (pbk.) | ISBN 9781315122717 (master ebook)
Subjects: LCSH: Leadership. | Executive coaching | Employees—Coaching of.
Classification: LCC HD57.7 (ebook) | LCC HD57.7 .E4176 2019 (print) | DDC 658.4/092—dc23
LC record available at https://lccn.loc.gov/2018034965

ISBN: 978-1-138-56494-7 (hbk)
ISBN: 978-1-138-56496-1 (pbk)
ISBN: 978-1-315-12271-7 (ebk)

Typeset in Times New Roman
by Apex CoVantage, LLC

MIX
Paper from responsible sources
FSC
www.fsc.org
FSC® C013056

Printed and bound in Great Britain by
TJ International Ltd, Padstow, Cornwall

To Etan and Jacob, two joyous gifts of learning.

Contents

Acknowledgements and thanks

Acknowledgements

With thanks to my two critical readers, Dr Susan Kahn and Sir Martin Donnelly KCB CMG, and to my Supervisor, Dr Anton Obholzer, who introduced me to the psychoanalytic approach.

Thanks

To the leaders and contributors who generously shared their stories, reflections and insights.

With thanks also for their help and expertise:

Alan Bookbinder, Holly Bookbinder, Dr Gerard Fromm, David Gittelson, Dr Peter Hawkins, Dr Caroline Horner, Dr Anthony Kazosi, Richard Laming, Dr Peter Hawkins, Dr Carole Pemberton, Dara Rigal, Dr Itamar Rogovsky and members of ISPSO.

About the author

Rachel Ellison's first career was in print and broadcast journalism. On one national newspaper, she observed the effect on employees of a commercially driven culture, which was run on fear. In a public service broadcast environment, she experienced values-led leadership. In both organisations it was imperative to create, innovate and deliver projects to tight deadlines.

Rachel joined the BBC as a multi-media news reporter, working on UK, European and international stories. After a stint on BBC Radio 4's Woman's Hour, Rachel was asked to create an equivalent programme for Afghan women. Its remit was to promote human rights, women's self-empowerment and conflict resolution. As programme editor, this was Rachel's first leadership role. She trained a team of 30 Afghan female journalists in Afghanistan, the former Soviet Union and in the UK. Within weeks of its launch, Afghan Woman's Hour, or Zan Wa Jahan Emrouzi (which is Dari for 'Woman in Today's World'), became one of the most listened to programmes in Afghanistan and the Afghan diaspora in Pakistan, Iran, the UK, Europe and the USA. *Men* wrote in to the programme to say how much they were learning from it too, including understanding better the needs of their wives, their mothers and their sisters.

Aged 36, Rachel was awarded an MBE *'for the promotion of human rights and the self-empowerment of women in Afghanistan'*. Her coaching style of leadership was recognised by the Director General of the BBC who awarded the programme BBC Team of the Year.

Whilst editor of Afghan Woman's Hour, Rachel volunteered to train as an executive leadership coach, on the BBC's internal coach training scheme. After leaving the BBC, she earned a master's degree in professional executive leadership coaching and set up her own company.

Rachel coaches C-suite leaders and emerging talent in global commercial, public and third sector organisations. Rachel coaches leaders in banking, electronics, the motor industry, retail and logistics, international diplomacy, health, law and development aid. Her clients include HSBC, the Bank of England, Boots Plc., Diageo, Hyundai, Samsung, the Foreign & Commonwealth Office, HM Treasury, Department for International Trade (Brexit), the BBC, the NHS, UK Sport, Teach First and UNICEF.

Rachel's coaching practice embraces international and multi-ethnic settings. It includes clients from more than 35 different cultures, including Afghanistan, Iraq, Syria, Sudan, Myanmar (Burma), China, Indonesia, Bolivia, Honduras, the former Soviet Union and countries in East, West and Southern Africa.

She is a visiting lecturer at Birkbeck University of London and an international public speaker. Rachel was awarded the 2018 Bridger Prize for 'the most original and creative paper' by ISPSO, the International Society for the Psychoanalytic Study of Organisations. The paper, on the psychological 'spaces' in a neonatal intensive care ward informed chapter 10 of this book: 'Comfort and Containment'.

Rachel has written numerous articles on coaching and is recognised as a thought leader and contributor to best practice, in the field of executive coaching and leadership. Rachel volunteers pro-bono for a number of charities concerned with health, education, women's and child's rights and international development.

This is Rachel's first book. It was inspired by some of her former coaching clients. Their experiences of leading through challenging, changing and sometimes dangerous situations is rich in learning and learning about leadership. Rachel believes their wisdoms have the potential to increase the quality of leadership in every sector of industry and organisational life.

Foreword

Dr Susan Kahn

International leadership and coaching: a global story

Rachel Ellison has written a book for the 21st century. Her rich and varied collection of global stories exposes leaders and coaches to the challenges of working in a complex and sometimes dangerous world. From war-torn Afghanistan to the Central African Republic, from an international supermarket chain to the inner sanctum of a neonatal intensive care unit, Ellison invites the reader to occupy and analyse these spaces.

In some chapters her own coaching clients describe the change to their leadership from the coaching encounter. Other chapters examine the profound impact of culture and politics. Through Phil, Claudia, Fatima and Jonny, we learn about the challenges of leaders in areas we might not be exposed to ourselves. We go inside a prison, a refugee camp, an NGO office in a conflict zone, even the parks and museums of the City of London.

We are invited into these intimate spaces and given the inside story on what it is like to lead and work in these different areas. As leaders we can understand, question and reflect on our own practice and as coaches we can consider a portfolio of needs beyond our own experience.

Ellison's style of writing is engaging and inviting. It is as if you are there. But she questions the actions of these leaders and interrogates them with a beneath the surface lens. What might be motivating these leaders? What might be going on beyond the structure and process of organisational life?

Ellison is not afraid to draw on her own experiences of important moments in life, sharing her own time as the mother of a premature baby in a neonatal intensive care unit. This privileged inside position is one many of us will not get a glimpse of, indeed we might be grateful for this and yet her analysis is without oversentimentality and allows us to examine a working environment that is so vital and yet so much out of our sight.

The book encourages us to think about how we would lead in situations alien to our own. How would we cope with the violence of an oppressive post-Taliban regime? How would be negotiate the violence and politics of prison life?

How would we ensure that cultural issues are managed productively in a retail environment?

Leaders and coaches should read this book and pause to consider the questions posed at the end of each chapter. Ellison urges us to think about the impact of our childhood on the coaches and leaders we become, to question our destructive behaviour and to develop greater self-awareness.

Who should read this book? Anyone who is interested in the complexities of working life, anyone who is curious about why leaders make the decisions they do, anyone who is coaching a client in a leadership position who wants to understand better what it might be like to function in an environment that has not been in the realms of their own experience.

This collection of inspiring and moving stories of leadership will transport you around the world. Candid and inviting, we learn about leadership challenges and triumphs; resistance and repetition; despair and hope. The book can be read from beginning to end or you can dip into each chapter as you choose. Each chapter can stand alone.

It is my pleasure to write this foreword and to recommend this book to you as one that will enrich you, encourage you to look awry at the working environment and to think about how you lead and how you coach your clients.

Susan Kahn, PhD, MSc, MA, BA is a consultant, corporate mediator, executive leadership coach and associate lecturer at Birkbeck, University of London.

Introduction

This book searches for excellence in leadership and coaching. It shares inspiring stories of leadership in multiple international and multi-cultural settings. It investigates effective leadership and explores what practices and behaviours generate creativity and resilience. It aims to provoke engagement and thinking that goes beneath the surface, through accounts from individuals, tasked with leading in varied, complex and sometimes highly challenging environments. Each chapter offers a study of an individual, a concept or an organisation, revealing the personal and professional growth of those involved.

The text attempts to offer original, fresh and courageous accounts of coming to work. Management dilemmas are explained and explored. As these experienced leaders share their career journeys, they enrich us with their honesty and humility, their openness to learn more about themselves and to develop their ability to lead. They communicate not just the stresses but their joy in coming to work.

Many but not all of the case studies featured here are former coaching clients. Some were leaders who chose to work with me. Others were assigned to me as their coach, as part of their organisation's global leadership development programme. Another was a receptionist at my local hairdresser. I met another contributor in a hospital. In the case of former coaching clients, I asked permission to interview them after their coaching programme had ended. Those who agreed to participate saw a chance to further their own professional development and, generously, to provide a learning opportunity for others.

Some consistent leadership themes emerge, such as resilience, change and economic uncertainty; resource cuts, managing diversity and role modelling; dealing with trauma and burn out. Other threads include creativity, innovation, organisational sustainability and eldership.

Whether working in a conflict zone or leading an elite high performance sports team, from retail to refugees, I focused mainly but not exclusively on two key questions:

- What does it take to be an effective leader in your field?
- What can the rest of us learn about leadership from you, even if we do a completely different kind of job?

The leaders and other contributors engage with these and other questions, intellectually, emotionally and intuitively. They bring perspectives from different cultures and different parts of the world, including Asia, Africa, Europe and America. Leaders explain the emotional and the practical challenges they face in their field of work. To their reflections, I bring additional psychological analyses and below the surface thinking. In reading this book, a lawyer or an accountant based in a big city can hear what it is like working in a refugee camp or in a supermarket context. Such diverse sources of learning offer a form of mindfulness and inner development that leaders can reinterpret and deploy in their own jobs.

Within this book there is also a call for higher ethics, greater diversity and improved sustainability in the way we work. I believe this has the potential to increase productivity, profit and fulfilment.

Organisations, groups and teams can flourish or fail, depending on the quality of leadership they are offered. This is a global story. It coincides with the compromising exposure of numerous commercial, public sector and third sector organisations, whose leaders' personal conduct misaligns with the integrity, values or imperative of their organisation.

Sound, ethical leadership of self-aware individuals creates an environment in which it is safe to voice and to challenge ideas. Healthy organisations attract talented people who want to stay. When staff are motivated and supportive of one another, they are less likely to call-in sick, to burn out or leave. Workers who are 'in flow' (Csikszentmihalyi 2008) create a stream of inspiring and enduring products for their customers. They also teach the next generation of leaders best practices on how to lead, how to serve and how to shape an organisation so that it is in good health for the long term.

Much of this book addresses senior leadership issues, but senior leaders also need to stay in touch and in tune with working life at the grassroots level. They risk compromising their professional and organisational success if they assume that the employee experience remains the same as when they started out in their careers. Being genuinely aware of who you are leading and how people respond to your leadership is critical.

You can read the chapters in this book in any order. Each chapter stands alone, surfacing leadership themes emerging from the narrative. Subheadings break up the text. This enables the busy and oft interrupted leader to concentrate and learn in short bursts, rather than feel they have insufficient time to embark on a large volume of prose. At the end of each chapter are questions for further reflection to encourage readers to integrate and apply ideas from this book when facing their next tricky work issue or important business decision.

Whilst focusing on leaders, this book is also designed to help executive coaches supporting those leaders, to search beneath the surface in their own and their client's thinking: To challenge harder.

Chapter 1 is about leading where it is hot, dusty and dangerous. It presents us with some of the leadership dilemmas and experiences of six international non-governmental development aid workers, posted to Somalia, Afghanistan,

Honduras, Senegal, the Central African Republic and the USA. Both personal and systemic patterns of behaviour are analysed. Everything a leader does and *doesn't* do sends a message to their team. Insights from NGO leaders include the need for humanitarian aid not just in war zones, but in every job and in every office, whatever the field of work. Organisations full of people supposedly 'doing good' can harbour abusive leaders who exploit their own staff and the needy whom they are ostensibly there to help.

Travelling the world cycling is a window into a different kind of leadership experience. Here the team is termed a collective, such is the diversity of disability of the para athletes within it. These individuals require intense empathy and bespoke management. The humility of this able-bodied leader accompanies the reader on a journey through what it is like to train, compete and manage people dealing with loss and pain.

Next we hear from another leader, also concerned with diversity, this time in a supermarket context. She decided she needed to relearn how to lead. Once admired and competent, her new job in the World Foods buying department of her company was so challenging that she found she could no longer achieve the results she was used to. Through rethinking her relationships with suppliers and staff she became an inspiration across the business and outside it too.

We stay with the theme of food and its potential role in conflict resolution. In this chapter, the sharing of recipes brought people out of entrenched assumption and prejudice into a stance where they started to recognise and share each other's similarity instead of difference.

Prejudice and cultural conditioning plays its part in a different way, with a Sudanese coaching client. This leader believed she had been allocated 'the worst coach'. That was me. I was the youngest coach and female. She assumed the 'best' coach was the male coach with white hair, because he was apparently the oldest coach. The client acknowledges and explores her culturally conditioned assumptions around status and quality.

The prisons chapter shows us a leader who defends the validity of every human being irrespective of perceived ability or status. Phil struggles with his own dysfunctional beginnings and is determined to offer convicted criminals the possibility of a pathway out of repetitive cycles of crime. His belief in education and vocation is part of his leadership strategy. When things go wrong inside a prison, Phil must manage violent and unpredictable situations. He is conscious that the way he leads in an emergency needs to enable and develop the capacity to lead, in the next generation of prison managers.

From being 'inside', to thinking outside the office, the next chapter takes us to a series of public spaces. This time with a coaching client who wrestles with his ability to think in a museum. Or a library. Or in an art gallery. Jonny notices his rebellious reactions to certain buildings and analyses how different locations impact his leadership and performance at work, his behaviour patterns and his thinking.

The chapter on refugees explores the emotional pain of being a witness to suffering. An individual but also a systemic lens is applied to consider the psychological desires and defences in play. We consider the testimony of a senior leader, a young volunteer worker and a member of a host community, experiencing an influx of refugees and internally displaced people.

Taking a different approach to the theme of internal displacement and psychological dislocation, we hear the perspective of a Czech teenager, watching the fall of Communism during the late 1980s and early 1990s. This chapter explores the psychological impact of oppressive leadership, the hypocrisy of obedience, secret capitalism and corruption.

Finally we move to an intimate, internal and exclusive space: The Neonatal Intensive Care Unit of a leading teaching hospital. As one would expect, the focus is on the baby and its parents. But the narrative also considers the impact on the medical teams supporting them, of being exposed to high levels of emotional distress, including dealing with high-risk life and death situations. This chapter explores the physical, metaphorical and psychological spaces in a hospital context. This chapter can be applied to other work settings, where the nature of the space and its influence on performance, outcomes and emotional wellbeing can be considered.

From politics to sport, humanitarian aid to cooking, what links these chapters is the diversity, curiosity and compassion of those who have shared their leadership journey and evidenced their desire to reflect, to grow, to learn and to create learning opportunities for others.

Every chapter of this book explores what constitutes high-quality leadership and what learning is transferable to other occupations.

If you are a leader, I hope this book provokes your thinking and illustrates how varied leadership challenges and successful leadership can be. I hope it helps you generate more ideas. I hope the questions I pose along the way travel with you beyond the reading of this book. Revisit anything that niggles you. In some way, it is calling for your attention.

For executive leadership coaches, challenge more. Take risks of creativity in your thought and in your questioning. Invite your clients to do the same. Be courageous. Be direct. But make sure you do sufficient work on your own emotional underpinnings before asking clients to dive deep on theirs.

This book presents leaders with the opportunity to lead with greater integrity and self-knowledge. It is about creating joy in how we work, for ourselves, for those we lead and those we serve in the course of our work. This book is an opportunity for leaders and executive coaches supporting those leaders to think deeply and honestly about their choices, their emotions and their behaviours.

Some names and organisations have been changed or anonymised.

Reference

Csikszentmihalyi, M. (2008). *Flow: The Psychology of Optimal Experience*. New York. Harper Collins.

Chapter 1

Leading where it's hot, dusty and dangerous

What commercial and public-sector leaders can learn about effective leadership from non-governmental development aid workers

> *People who lose the connection between the individual and the policy level can be sucked into one story . . . as I was. Our most effective leaders have compassion. They are moved by the story, not paralysed by it.*

It is interesting to consider what it takes to work in a war zone. Or where extremes of climate, poverty or corruption make doing one's job particularly difficult. Of concern is how leaders stay resilient and prevent burn out in themselves and in those they lead. How do leaders stay inspired and committed to their job? How do they achieve authenticity and insight?

This chapter is based on interviews with a number of former coaching clients working for an international non-governmental development aid organisation. Their stories take us to Somalia, Afghanistan and Honduras; then to the USA, the Central African Republic and Senegal.

I asked them two key questions:

- What does it take to be an effective leader where it is hot, dusty and dangerous?
- What can other leaders learn from leaders working with such extremes of human emotion and experience?

This chapter includes themes such as ego-free leadership, conflict, violence and belief in the customer. There are examples of collaboration, role modelling and deliberate but also inadvertent reward.

There are multiple opportunities to interpret what may be going on individually and organisationally through looking beneath the surface or taking a psychoanalytic approach. This chapter considers working with crisis, uncertainty, ambiguity and vulnerability. It looks at how leaders lead and develop others, holding in mind the vulnerability of their core customer – millions of the world's poorest children. Many of these leaders carry high ethical principles, yet their work requires them to navigate corrupt individuals and failing systems.

I asked these third sector leaders what advice they would give employees working for big corporations, small start-ups and the public sector.

I encourage you to reflect on what inspires you about these stories and to ask questions of yourself and your organisation; to challenge yourself to lead differently and more effectively – from a human and a profits perspective.

Leading where it's hot, dusty and dangerous: what commercial and public-sector leaders can learn about effective leadership from non-governmental development aid workers

As a coach to some of the most experienced non-governmental development aid workers in the world, I began reflecting on what it takes to be an effective leader working in extremely challenging environments. Thousands of aid agency staff are posted to humanitarian missions around the globe. Conditions can be physically and emotionally tough. Employees expect to spend whole careers moving from region to region, working amidst disease epidemics, famine and social disadvantage; they work in countries enduring natural disaster, political instability or civil war. They work with the poor. They work with the displaced. Such leaders are often highly values led, resilient and compassionate people. Inevitably, some third sector leaders are corrupt, disillusioned and abusive, but a great many of them display the qualities associated with 'servant leadership', constantly thinking what they can do to enrich, care for and help others, before benefiting themselves.

Somalia: ego-free leadership in a war zone

These are my people. I am responsible for them. I cannot leave. I am their leader.

Fatima stayed. The compound where she worked in Mogadishu, the Somali capital, was stormed by gunman, following two car bombs which went off outside the gates. Fifteen people died. Fatima and her staff were under siege for two hours. Fatima, a senior leader with regional responsibility for a team of local and international employees, was born into the Masai tribe in Tanzania but converted to Christianity. When crisis struck, she evacuated her international staff. Next on the list would have been herself. But she didn't go.

> *Where can my local staff flee to? This is their home, their country. They are not safe here in Somalia, but I'm not allowed to evacuate them to Kenya under our emergency protocol, because they are not classified as 'internationals' like the rest of my staff.*

This display of leadership moved most who heard about it. Working in Somalia, Fatima lives thousands of miles away from her husband and children. She has rights. The right to try to protect her own life. The right to an organisational protocol for emergencies. Bombs going off right outside the office certainly counts as a hostile emergency. But Fatima still chose to stay put. To honour her idea of what leadership means for her.

Let's consider whether Fatima's behaviour was a brave example of ego-free leadership, or whether it was masochistic or reckless.

In a cultural reflection, members of the African Masai tribe have a reputation for being strong warriors. I wonder whether Fatima's decision not to evacuate herself embodied an ancient tribal construct around staying with 'your own people' when under attack. Looking after others as you would like to be treated is also a Judeo-Christian principle. Doing the 'right thing' is part of collective or community responsibility in many other cultures too. We do not know for certain, but I hypothesise that for Fatima, despite her conversion to Christianity, deeper cultural traditions are in play.

The interpretation of Fatima's behaviour as ego-free may, in fact, be faulty. Perhaps she was operating with her ego fully engaged. Doing good can also make *you* feel good; important, elated, even more 'alive'. After all, if she evacuates herself to safety leaving most of her team behind, she may have to confront the inevitable fact that she is no longer a leader. At least, not a leader of this particular team. This may compromise her sense of self and her professional identity. Indeed, had she abandoned her team, as per her organisational protocol, would she have felt too guilty or too ashamed to lead that or any team again? Her decisions may be about pride.

There may be other ego-driven factors at work here. Perhaps Fatima remained with her staff out of loyalty to the idea of what leadership means to her, or because of the pain the act of leaving her team would cause her. We might also consider the systemic apartheid of which human lives are valuable enough to fly to safety and which are not. It would be difficult for any organisation to draw this line perfectly, for evacuating staff then calls into consideration protecting their families as well. The costs and logistics would spiral out of control.

I am curious about whether Fatima's refusal to leave was a conscious or unconscious attempt to obtain recognition. Her decision to stay meant that she risked personal suffering or even martyrdom. As a consequence, she may now be famous in her organisation. Such individual acts of courage by its leaders may be stored in a corporate memory bank at HQ, or on the contrary, in very large organisations they may barely register, or be denied – stored safely out of sight. If inconvenient, memory of such actions or behaviours may even be required to evaporate.

Fatima's humanitarian decision made within an organisation with a humanitarian remit comes with a dilemma. On the one hand her leadership is admired, but on the other, it may be imperative that the system does not appear to reward, praise or encourage via inadvertent or explicit incentive, such as role modelling, behaviours which involve danger or a risk to a leader's life.

If Fatima had evacuated herself, she may have found it difficult to psychologically tolerate what she had left behind. Likewise, the staff she evacuated may have complex feelings about the colleagues who could not join them. Might there perhaps be some form of abandonment story in Fatima's past that influenced her decision making in the moment? We may not know the exact thinking behind Fatima's decision, but what is important here is to generate the inquiry.

Let us consider some additional beneath the surface or psychoanalytically informed ideas. I wonder if Fatima's decision to stay represents the attachment she has to her work community or her work identity. Her lack of self-importance and her commitment to what is good and right, from her perspective.

It could be the opposite. An egotistical attachment to 'me me me'. To being the saviour leader. A messianic manager who risks her own safety and even her career to *save her people*. Fatima may offer a symbol of female leadership, or even mothering. It could be that Fatima's maternal instinct was squashed or sublimated, such that what we see on the surface is a leader refusing to self-evacuate. But what is subconsciously driving this is the instinct to care for the team – the team she may have even 'given birth' to. It is intriguing to consider whether we would arrive at a similar analysis had Fatima been a man. Senior leadership carries with it a version of parenting or shepherding, whether offered by a man or a woman. We do not know whether a man presented with the same dilemma would make the same decision as Fatima. Nor whether he would feel a similar level of emotional intensity at such a choice point.

It would be understandable for any leader to feel torn in a situation like this, with both a desire to flee and feelings of guilt for doing so. Especially when escaping involves leaving others behind who are also in danger. This notion of feeling conflicted or 'split' appears in other case studies in this book. Splitting can be a defence against anxiety. But it is not usually a psychologically healthy option for the long term. The difficulty of making the right decisions, remaining resilient during times of stress or distress and staying whole as a person, rather than ending up cut off from one's emotions, is a challenge for many leaders dealing with emergencies and suffering. That suffering can be corporate as well as humanitarian. We see later in this chapter that humanitarian aid can be needed in the dullest of offices, not just in conflict zones.

Another approach for Western readers of this book is to consider what is culturally embedded for many Asian communities and also in Eastern, Central and some parts of Southern Africa: The concept of the collective. One thinks in terms of the community first, rather that one's own individual perspective. In Fatima's situation there is the clash of the 'I' stance with the 'we'; the ego ideal of making leadership decisions that feel like the 'right thing to do' versus what is corporately deemed appropriate behaviour. There is the collision of self-interest with concern for others' needs. Fatima's dilemma represents a kind of unintended apartheid – an emotional tangle within, as she thought about what to do.

A Western leader might have a more individualistic approach. It is also worth considering who makes the rules in Fatima's organisation – and from what cultural approach decisions about emergency protocols are reached.

Perhaps Fatima unconsciously embodied the feelings of the colleagues she evacuated. We may never know what her ex-pat team projected onto her in terms of an expectation of mothering or protection. Nor how her local family of staff felt about her decision. It would be interesting to know if Fatima identified more strongly with her local Somali staff, rather than with the 'family' that is her organisation. It was a polarised choice. She couldn't half-stay.

Somalia: ego-free leadership in a war zone

Reflections for leaders

- What do you think of Fatima's dilemma to stay or to leave?
- When have you been forced to make polarised choices as a leader?
- Do you have an example of when you led 'ego-free'?
- When have you stood by your people when 'under fire'?
- Can you think of examples of metaphorical 'martyrdom' in your organisation?
- Attachment to community – what kind of community do you seek to create at work?

Reflections for coaches

- Dealing with an emergency – consider examples from work or home life
- Entangled decision making – compromise and guilt . . .
- Polarised choices
- Exploring the maternal or paternal instinct in a leader
- What communities is the client attached to?

Afghanistan: stripping off the grime that's holding you back

> *Coaching is like cleaning your pots. If you scrub them really hard, so they're really clean, they cook better, faster and more efficiently. It burns less energy.*
>
> [Indian proverb]

Ashima, who works for an international children's aid agency in Kabul, evaluates the benefits to her of executive leadership coaching, linking it to an Indian saying. Ashima is married with two university age sons. Nearing the end of her career, this is the first time she has been offered executive leadership coaching. It is also the first time in her career that her professional learning has focused not on operational excellence but on developing herself as a leader.

This is what she noticed was changing: An increase in energy, efficiency, insight and presence. Because her day job was so busy, Ashima did not think she had time to explore her leadership style or her meaning and purpose in coming to work. At first she approached coaching like a chore:

> *It's about stripping off the grime that's holding you back from being more efficient and effective. In psychological terms, you have to be prepared to explore the uncomfortable side of your emotions, not stay at the transactional level of the day-to-day job.*

Ashima leads an international team working in a conflict zone. It is a highly stressful foreign posting, where families cannot join. Everyone lives and works together in one of several international compounds. The buildings are surrounded by 20-foot-high concrete walls, laced with rolls of razor wire. Because of the risk of kidnap and bombings, employees may not shop for food, go for a walk, saunter through the local markets or go out for a bit of sightseeing. There are no sites to see anyway. They were all destroyed. The legendary almond trees and trickling brooks of Afghan literature are now firewood and parched river beds.

You can workout at the gym inside the safe house. Or go in a vehicle convoy to an ex-pat-filled restaurant. Apart from that, all your meals are cooked for you. Your washing is done for you too. This might sound luxurious, but it's a restricted life, leaving little to do but work. Many people find it insular, physically frustrating and emotionally lonely.

Inside the compound is a mix of people from one culture, posted to another culture. Employees are answerable simultaneously to two customers: A nation of traumatised and impoverished women and children, and the bosses at headquarters in New York – a place perceived to be as relentlessly political, rather white, rather male and rather European in attitude. Ashima describes her remit:

> *We're trying to bring basic human rights not just to children in Afghanistan, but to their parents and grandparents too. Water, sanitation, vaccination programmes, schooling – especially to girls.*

There is a lot to learn when working in a conflict zone, as I had found out for myself ten years earlier in Kabul, where I led a team of Afghan female staff, derived from 18 different national tribes. Each tribe has its own language, traditional dress, social codes and distinct melding of Islamic and Afghan customs. I was a BBC news reporter who had migrated to human rights, conflict resolution and development aid work.

Afghanistan is a nation of people who have endured three decades of war, followed by a six-year drought. There is a generation of lost learning, with schools closed because of the political volatility. At the time I was working there, shortly after the Taliban had fallen, jobs were few, because nearly everything was imported from Pakistan. I saw a downward spiral of skills and poverty, unemployment and domestic frustration, including violence against women.

Nearly everybody – even the most educated and privileged – suffered some form of post-traumatic stress disorder. My employee's resilience could oscillate in a moment from unfalteringly tough, to emotionally fragile, even psychologically unstable. Recurring nightmares meant performance at work was inconsistent. Leaders themselves were traumatised whilst attempting to manage others also experiencing unresolved grief, trauma or flashbacks.

Fathers and brothers would chaperone my female staff to work. The women were often late because of the traffic, an unmade road, a washed out road [for parched though Afghanistan is in the summer, it can be muddy, flooded or snow blocked for months during the winter] and the paucity of public transport. A member of the team might turn up late to the office because of a jealous husband. An unemployed man who relies on his wife's entrepreneurialism for income but feels so humiliated by her success may hit her.

Violence in Afghan society is well known and even accepted. This includes violence between men and women but also violence by women towards other, often younger or lower status, women. One wonders what unconscious process is playing out where a mother-in-law beats her daughter-in-law. Husbands exemplify taking back their dominant position, through beating their wives or children. Whilst not condoning such behaviour in any way it is worth noting that in both male and female perpetrated violence, self-hatred rather than hatred of another may be being expressed.

With thousands of war widows and a loss of skills through political upheaval and lack of education, the chance of a getting job and a vital source of income can be scarce. The radio programme I created began with a team of one, gradually expanding to a group of 30 Afghan women journalists. Some could not read or write. But I believed they could all find and record vivid human stories.

One morning one of my staff did not turn up for work. She had been hit so violently by her husband that she miscarried a baby none of us knew she was expecting. My translator told me that her vagina was hanging down on the outside of her body; her teeth were scattered across the kitchen floor. The husband, it was explained to me, feels humiliated by his own lack of employment whilst his wife is proving successful in the workplace. This shocking example teaches us a great deal.

This is an example of the collision of Western, Islamic and ancient Afghan culture, concerning the right or even financial imperative of women to go to work. This collision is complicated further by the encouragement of educated Afghan women to attain PhD's in Russia and speak foreign languages, whilst remaining submissive within their marriages. For poor or widowed women, working is essential in order to eat. These women may have no other source of income, yet attempting to earn some money confuses the psychological dynamics of the established group or family.

The violence – a smashed laptop computer in one case, a smashed up woman in another – is by no means a unique situation in an Afghan context. It is worth reflecting on the systemic impotence, which may be felt by men who find their loss of social status unbearably shameful. Such notions of a rightful level of power do not solely apply in post-conflict zones and emerging economies. Whilst some circumstances heighten the likelihood of domestic violence, such behaviour is an international issue which does not discriminate between rich or poor, the educated or illiterate.

When this particular colleague was beaten up, I was a fairly young, fairly new leader. I did not know how to handle the situation. My line manager was thousands of miles away in a different time zone. I didn't have a coach. There was no safe space for me to take my feelings and reflect on what to do. I was certainly unable to coach myself at that stage. The work was intense, deadline driven, energising and exhausting. There was little time to think who to turn to for guidance.

I grappled with the dilemma of whether to continue to employ this member of my team, lest it risk further or increased levels of violence at home. I was conscious of managing my own emotions and appropriately leading my distraught staff who had to translate immensely personal information into English for me. Also to consider was whether I was receiving and understanding the full translation of events, or whether some facts were being censored because they were culturally 'unsayable'. Sometimes a person will give a stranger from a different culture a fuller picture of what's going on than they would if speaking to a fellow national. In front of a translator from their own culture, it is common for people to want to save face. They fear being judged, and thus hide some of the facts. An additional consideration is the issue of translating versus interpreting. I would frequently be told what my team thought I wanted to hear. That is not the same as translating what was actually said. So, obtaining the truth can be hindered. Whilst translation is greatly appreciated, it means no conversation is truly private. Imagine the impact of not being able to have a private word with your boss.

We return to the leadership dilemma of what to do regarding my seriously injured employee: If I continue to pay her, I might empower this woman to go back to work, towards a safer, perhaps independent future. Her job would give her self-confidence and money. Alternatively, it may provoke further marital violence, including putting this member of my team at risk of losing her children, should her husband decide to divorce her. Under Islamic law, when a man divorces his wife, non-breastfeeding children usually become his property.

So, a woman can leave. But often, though not always, without her children. I kept asking myself:

> *What behaviours am I rewarding? What behaviours am I role modelling? What values am I trying to uphold as a leader of my team?*

For me, leading in such extreme conditions means developing significant emotional resilience, whilst retaining compassion, flexibility and cultural awareness. Working out how to protect oneself against burn out is important. Otherwise a leader risks failing to complete a project or a posting, leaving their team with a series of constantly changing leaders, or with no leader at all.

I did not feel I successfully resolved the situation with that particular female reporter. I felt ill-equipped as a leader and as a person. The Internet was a less developed resource than it is today. And in any case, there wasn't necessarily enough electricity or sufficient signal to run a computer or access the world wide web at that time, in that location. I decided to give my talented and conscientious employee as much control as I could. Her circumstances were unfolding publicly and also remotely, for this mother of four children lived a day's journey from the office. Our translated conversations took place over crackling and intermittent telephone lines. This made them even less intimate. Even less private.

In leadership terms, perhaps such situations are not possible to resolve cleanly, especially in a country where the rule of law may not be upheld. How congruent this incident seemed with the very remit of the women's radio programme we were trying to make – that of increasing awareness of human rights, improving women's self-empowerment, education and contributing to conflict resolution.

What happened to my employee, and its effect on me and my team of women reporters, is a glimpse of what many NGO workers, like Ashima, deal with every day. As well as exposure to direct frustrations and dangers, they are also affected indirectly by the trauma of others:

> *These conditions make you feel far more alive as a human being. You're less narrow minded, less concerned with pettiness – there is less anger. I don't correct others now in the way that I would have done before.*

From dust and dirt, to heat and cold, failing electricity generators and water cuts that last for hours every day; from political instability to violence in the home – these are some of the challenges which explain why some of the most fascinating jobs in the world are termed 'hardship postings'.

Ashima has adjusted her management style in response to the harshness of the environment:

> *As a leader, you have to temper what you ask of people in these conditions. In our organisation, we need to be mindful about demanding results and delivery when our staff are working in such stressful conditions. Your colleagues are your family. In a recent attack on the Indian embassy and then a restaurant, here in Kabul, colleagues and friends were killed.*
>
> *My team was traumatised and in shock. I couldn't just ask them to get on with their day job. You have to decide, prioritise, drop deadlines and hope that the head office understands that something might be a bit late. Everything is always an exceptional circumstance in a conflict zone.*

Ashima extends her compassionate, values-based principles to include not only those in need of development aid but also those delivering it. This represents an evolution for Ashima's leadership style, which attempts to counter an unpredictable, chaotic and sometimes ruthless work setting:

> *I try to be neutral, impartial, to support people working here. I remind myself of the personal and family sacrifices employees are making, to do the work of an international non-governmental organisation here.*
>
> *Leading a team in a place like Kabul reaffirms that there is no place for ego as a manager or in life. You have to have the capacity for deep empathy. I absorb a lot. Yet my husband is hundreds of miles away in another country, so as a leader here, I sometimes feel very alone.*

Afghanistan: stripping off the grime that's holding you back

Reflections for leaders

- When do you need to temper what you demand of your staff?
- High walls and razor wire . . . what could be preventing your people seeing what is going on 'outside'?
- What are the potential consequences of extreme stress on ideas, vision and performance?

Reflections for coaches

- What is this leader's equivalent of grimy cooking pots?
- Post-traumatic stress disorder (PTSD) – clarify what the symptoms of this are and whether you may be coaching someone managing their own PTSD or someone else's
- What organisational structures are in place should an employee be suffering from PTSD?
- Do you need to refer your client to an appropriate source of professional help e.g. trained trauma counsellor or psychotherapist? You may not be trained nor therefore 'safe' to handle this yourself?

Honduras

> *Everything in Honduras is solved by killing. If you have a dispute over a property, it's solved by killing. If you argue with a neighbour, it's solved by killing. There is narco-traffic and kidnap. People don't talk to each other. They solve it with killing.*

My client messaged me minutes before our coaching session was due to begin:

> *I'm sorry, I can't make our coaching session today because of a narco-traffic shooting in one of our rural projects.*

This is one of the more original excuses I've heard for rescheduling a Skype call!

Ordinary people struggle on, with aid agencies trying to reach the most vulnerable communities, especially children. International staff say they become, disillusioned, tired and burnt out. That is why many agencies have a policy of shorter postings here. Such is the exhaustion that these already resilient employees experience in Honduras. They say the environment drains them of energy. Maybe this mirrors how some Hondurans feel: they might like to be transferred to somewhere safer, where living is relaxing rather than terrifying. Where problems are solved by talking, not killing.

War is a form of leadership done through the killing model. Whilst Honduras is not officially at war, killing in this society is another 'normal'. The idea of helping or trying to repair a repeated cycle of trauma may not necessarily be greeted as helpful. The idea of outside agencies imposing their own leadership values may even add to the sense of damage being felt by ordinary people or the system. Perhaps that is why this damage is then transferred on to aid agency staff, expressed as depressive hopelessness and exhaustion.

I wonder what foreign aid organisations can do when members of their staff react with such consistency to a particular situation or region. How do leaders lead differently in one tricky part of the world compared to another? Visibility may be relevant. There may be a greater sense of empathy from the head office, friends and family when your work is understood because it is *visible* – because it is on the news. This leader's emphasis on the child in all of this may be a subconscious attempt to shift out of the kill-kill model, and focus on a 'third thing', to shift the emphasis from enmity and opposites towards a shared goal or a shared source of compassion.

> *To be a successful leader in Honduras, you have to be prepared to speak up for children in the face of the constant threat of violence and everyday indifference, or even corruption. With all this going on, it's hard to motivate your staff – but you have to have hope, and keep going.*

Maybe this leader feels like the 'child' herself, helpless unless a 'grown up', or adult, does something to change things. Whilst we might assume that seeking to help actual children is a good thing, it can also provoke envy from those who are not children but also feel they desperately need some form of 'help'. In addition, the supposed helpers, may render childlike those they are trying to assist, thus creating more troubled children, rather than fewer. So the aid workers who express their exhaustion and hopelessness may be offering us data about what a whole city or country's 'system' may be experiencing.

Honduras

Reflections for leaders

- How are people metaphorically 'killing' each other in your organisation, i.e. ideas, projects?
- Does how you feel reflect how your customers might be feeling?
- Who is prepared to speak up in your organisation, even when it feels 'dangerous' to do so?
- Where is there silence in your organisation . . . where maybe there shouldn't be?
- Who or what areas of the business receive little or no attention?

Reflections for coaches

- What data is not being 'seen' by the leader or by their organisation?
- What issues receive little or no 'air time'?
- Help your leader explore what the system might be communicating, through accessing his own, or indeed your (the coach's) own, feelings
- What transference do you experience when your client responds to these questions?

The USA and Central African Republic

How many meetings include the question: 'But will HQ say "yes"?'

Dominique is a humanitarian rights expert, posted to New York where her international non-governmental aid organisation has its headquarters. HQ is an environment perceived by many as white, male and European. It feels bureaucratic, hierarchical, rigid and stunting of creative ideas. The atmosphere seems fearful rather than enabling. This does not appear congruent with the mission stations, which are usually bursting with humanitarian endeavour and nimble, responsive decision making. How disappointing for the many field workers, who must win approval from the hub so that they can help their most important customers: Vulnerable children.

If New York doesn't say *'yes'*, aid workers in the field cannot initiate new rescue packages for girls and boys in their region. Even if they believe that this is what will really make a difference to their lives, or even the difference in these children *being* alive.

The agonising tug of politics at the head office appears, to the outsider, to be at odds with the highly committed, values-led leaders aching to reach out to children in the villages of Africa and Asia, Indonesia and India. However, the cool detachment of those based in the headquarters building may serve to calm or still the panic and chaos of emotions, which can swirl around even the most grounded of field workers dealing with an emergency. There are practical considerations. Namely the competing demands on money, staff and resources amidst simultaneously deserving causes in every region of the world. Dominique is based in New York:

> *Our most effective leaders have compassion. They are moved by the story, not paralysed by it.*

Dominique recalls a recent field trip to the Central African Republic – a war-torn country of 4.5 million[1] people, bordered by Sudan, Chad, the Democratic Republic of Congo and Cameroon:

> *Every night I cried in my hotel room. During the day, these women came to tell me that they are being raped four or five times a month. I'm meant to*

come up with humanitarian aid policies. Rape is being used systematically, as a weapon of war. And I can't do anything to help these women and stop it. I just cried and cried.

Whether at head office or in the field, leadership in many aid agencies is fundamentally about motivation not money. Dominique explains that the most effective leaders, in her view, have compassion:

They are moved by the story, not paralysed by it. They then take the individual woman's problem and go to the big vision and bigger issues. Yet they still see the connection between the individual and a large-scale policy decision.

On one occasion Dominique once became so distressed by a situation that she witnessed on a foreign posting, she considered resigning and retraining as a doctor:

I just wanted to help that one woman. To heal a sick person. To beat up the man who raped her. To save her life. To know whose life I had saved.

People who lose the connection between the individual and the policy level, can be sucked into one story – as Dominique was. Alternatively, they risk becoming lost in the processing of policy documents and meetings about policy documents. Workers in development aid have to live with the fact that often they cannot see the difference they are making to individuals. They do not know whose life they may have saved.

The best aid agency leaders retain the connection between who they are trying to help, why and how best to do that. They try not to split off from their own emotions nor allow parts of their team or organisation to disconnect. They are able to find a way to tolerate the pain of what they are leading through, without losing empathy. They work hard and consciously not to be consumed by the story in front of them, in order to continue being able to lead effectively through it.

It is a balance. Connection, compassion and rivetted detachment[2] appears to be the way to cope. Some protocols may seem boring or even obstructive. But aid workers must keep themselves physically safe and emotionally protected first, in order to help others next. Back at the head office, these leaders' leaders need to have a sophistication of understanding and the ability to trust. To know that a national or international initiative, informed by field workers, will fulfil the imperative to change vulnerable people's lives for the better.

The USA and Central African Republic

Reflections for leaders

- When have you become so emotionally involved in something going on at work that you were sucked in?

- When was your reaction the opposite i.e., you disconnected?
- Politically, who are people anxious to please in your organisation, when it is not the customer?
- Silences in your organisation: When are there instances of people 'screaming' but the organisation cannot tolerate what they are communicating/asking for?

Reflections for coaches

- Employees becoming consumed by a situation and thus passionate but possibly less able to lead effectively or objectively
- Splitting off parts of the organisation from itself or its employees
- Leading with 'rivetted detachment'

New York, USA: collaboration and role modelling when it's hot, dusty and dangerous

> *You need to communicate to excite. That means excite and thus engage multiple constituents so that you can amplify impact through collaboration.*

Mita is Ivy League and Oxbridge educated. The daughter of ambitious Bangladeshi parents who were convinced that educational opportunity, would provide a platform for Mita's future successes. Mita cannot help but combine her own empathic feelings as a mother with her experiences of literally carrying some of the world's most disempowered and vulnerable children. She has been posted to Vietnam, Ethiopia and Kenya:

> *To be a leader in this field takes passion and compassion. You have to have passion for the mission – which is to think of children first. You need to embrace and adapt to different cultures and different situations. You need to communicate to excite.*

Mita emphasises her point:

> *Always know that there is more that can be done. Celebrate successes but remember the last child has yet to be reached and supported.*

This is all very convincing from an aid worker's point of view. But what takeaways can such insights offer today's commercial or public-sector leader? Mita offers this:

> *It's not always about oneself and about profit. There is richness in diversity. People live in the real world where there are so many different factors which*

impinge on everyday life. It's worth it for the commercial leader to take the time to try to understand this [in service of more effective outcomes for the company, longer term].

Indeed, you do not have to be an aid worker to see how often people go to great lengths to deliver on a project for work, staying in the office late, sacrificing time with their partner or family, or even their own health, through travel, stress, eating poorly and not exercising.

So non-humanitarian aid workers may in fact be making humanitarian sacrifices. This can mean sacrificing their needs. Or sacrificing the wellbeing of others, through inappropriate demands at work or at home through poor leadership or bullying. Not to mention projecting frustration and pressure onto loved ones after office hours. We could interpret scenarios where tiredness and poor management lead to victimhood at work and the transference of this pressure onto more junior staff or relationships outside work. You do not have to be somewhere dusty and dangerous, to experience genuine stress or even distress in a job. Such transportation of suffering may or may not be accompanied by apparent indifference – be that interpersonal or systemic. Mita has some advice for commercial leaders:

Commercial leaders might think less about competition and more about what can be done together. In other words, seek to collaborate with other agencies – internal and external – in order to be more effective and deliver better results.

There are less obvious, indirect ways for companies and public-sector organisations to deliver Corporate Social Responsibility, now termed Corporate Social Value. Every leader and those they are leading, can contribute to the betterment of humanity in some way. Be that inside the workplace or in the wider community.

It might simply be thinking more deeply about the impact of how you lead, rather than purely looking at the business results you achieve. I think optimal leadership which includes values-conscious decision making, is a path to higher profit, productivity and organisational sustainability. What need to shift in many organisations are the targets which create an incentive for leaders to think one or two quarters ahead, rather than reward them for thinking which delivers better results years into the future.

New York, USA: collaboration and role modelling when it's hot, dusty and dangerous

Reflections for leaders

- What connection is it important for you to see, when doing your job?
- How could you bring more humanity to the way your team works?
- Thinking about what stances or views need amplifying – yours, others', the organisation's?

Reflections for coaches

- What humanitarian sacrifices may this leader be making?
- What humanitarian sacrifices may this leader be causing others to make?
- How might these sacrifices represent or make up for problems being experienced by society as a whole or by a particular industry sector?
- What leadership behaviours need amplifying?

Senegal: factional splitting, corruption and reward

> *Understand and know your team. Business leaders need to go beyond the formal, and understand the informal power centres . . . Everything you do and everything you don't do sends a signal.*

Simon leads multiple teams of international and local staff. An MBA graduate with a PhD in engineering from the University of Cambridge in the UK, Simon worked in big business before joining an international aid agency. He is accustomed to bloody conflict. His current posting sees him in charge of 24 countries across Central Africa. There is usually a humanitarian emergency, or even a civil war, developing on his patch.

Simon believes leading in an international aid context, in which people are rarely sacked for poor performance and there are no financial bonuses available to reward exceptional performance, offers the commercial leader much, in terms of technique and focus. Themes include: Role modelling and reward behaviours, prior analysis and multi-point negotiation, scenario planning in the face of significant instability and setbacks, failure and resilience.

Simon explains:

> *In order to make a deal in a non-profit context, you have to do a lot of figuring out. You need to spend time seeking to understand and know your team. Business leaders must go beyond the formal, and understand the informal power centres at play.*
>
> *Some employees come from the political class; they might be on the lowest salary level but in their country these are important people. So I spend lots of time working out how to hit each person's buttons or drivers. If you only understand your agenda, you'll fail. It's about using softer ways to reward staff and motivate people to come into the office with a spring in their step.*

Employees need to feel genuinely recognised by a leader who believes that each person in the team has something to contribute. Those leaders need to lead by example, earning rather than assuming respect and being seen to treat everyone in the team equally. This can help avoid the development of cliques of in-people and out-people.

It is important for staff to see their senior leaders facing up to problems that need to be dealt with.

For example, in Simon's team there was a case of an international employee who had been in-country for 12 years instead of the standard five years. He was holding the rest of the team, including the boss, hostage. Simon believes that everything you do and everything you don't do sends a signal:

> *People like this are likely to have built their little empire; often they'll have several businesses running on the side that everyone knows about. These are clear abuses of position. When you're the new head of the office, do you seek to understand it, do you turn a blind eye, or do you tackle it?*

Another example might be a poor performer, someone who's not doing their job well and making other people in the team unhappy as a consequence. One solution might be to find an exit strategy, such as actively helping that person find a new job that is a better fit for their skills and competencies.

Strong and skilled negotiation techniques are another crucial aspect of being an effective leader in an international aid organisation. Simon explains:

> *Commercial negotiation is very valuable, refined, rational; it has a calculable technique, e.g. the walk-away price. The targets usually have numbers on them. You can go in well prepared and achieve win-win outcomes on both sides.*

But in a development aid or humanitarian crisis context, negotiations can be more complex and multidimensional. Finding solutions requires a deeper understanding of the differences in objectives on both sides. Much greater creativity may be required. What is at stake is sometimes less quantifiable and potentially highly political. Success is determined by prior analysis and preparation for the negotiation, figuring out the stakes and packaging multi-point negotiations in the discussions. The classic *'we want this, for which we'll offer that'* approach is too simplistic. Going in on a single axis risks failure early on. It is unlikely to land a deal. But multiple trades enable a win-win.

One might expect similar behaviour in international commercial negotiations. But some commercial leaders take a blunter approach. They hold an adversarial stance, i.e. '*how do I get a bigger slice of the cake?*' Ideally, within the restrictions of anti-competition laws and conflicts of interest, companies could try to collaborate more, to make the *whole* cake bigger – that way everyone sells more and profits go up. A similar approach could be used within organisations. Interdepartmentally, there are opportunities being lost because of a failure to work together and think together, in service of greater joint successes.

Returning to the international aid agency context, leaders must constantly plan for instability in their region. Yet they cannot resource every possibility all the time, because it costs too much money. So a significant amount of thinking goes into scenario planning. For example, a dramatic spike in cholera, when there may not have been a cholera case in an area for years. Many people could die. Simon faced a situation where he had to plan for a potential outbreak of disease across 24 different countries in Africa. This is what he learned:

> *The key is being nimble, turning the whole emergency plan around 180 degrees, because you predicted events wrongly. Beneath that is having the mechanisms in place to reverse earlier decisions or plans quickly. That means investment up front. For example, establishing early and accurate surveillance systems really counts with an outbreak of an infectious disease. If you can react early, you can contain the spread. That means fewer lives will be lost.*

So, mindfulness around the allocation of resources at the planning stage, can determine crucial differences in outcomes and options later. How many times do leaders express their weariness with having to be reactive rather than proactive? In a humanitarian aid context, leaders must be able to mobilise, focus and refocus all their teams at a moments' notice. We can apply such dexterity of thinking in a business context: Leaders need to be less linear in their thinking. Their organisations need to foresee change: To be able to rise above the frantic pace of the everyday and see the helicopter view. Take the photographic film company Kodak for example. Once a world leader in its field, it failed to foresee the shift to digital photography format fast enough. Its core business rapidly collapsed and Kodak filed for bankruptcy .

Whether it concerns a public health crisis or anticipating social unrest, humanitarian aid workers are exposed to a high degree of extreme stress, setbacks, frustrations and sometimes failure. The associated emotions and toll on the body can be intense. Leaders need to become adept at self-management, encouraging their staff to develop these skills too. It helps to digest disappointments and bring an attitude of learning, in response to setbacks – then move on. Conscious, reflective leadership such as this can limit the transfer of stress onto others, either at work or at home. It can help dissipate the impact of handling multiple pressures, e.g. from government authorities, rebel groups or organisational headquarters, whilst dealing with an emergency.

Empathy and flexibility are critical to helping your team through difficult situations:

> *Your team is not a homogenous group. Some people are by nature calmer than others under stress. You may need to temporarily redeploy who does what.*

Not only must Simon deal with outbreaks of infectious disease in his region, but he is required to manage effectively amidst political contagion too. In humanitarian crises, a national conflict can play out in your organisation or across your team. Local staff may come into conflict with each other during meetings, splitting along opposing tribal lines. It is therefore imperative for leaders to understand the culture in which they are operating. They must spot such factional divisions. Or better still, anticipate its potential to polarise the team or even destroy previously good rapport between colleagues. Leaders must try to mitigate against this ahead of time. Simon goes into a state akin to hypervigilance during some emergencies.

> *You have to watch yourself and everything going on around you – like a film – from the outside.*

Senegal: factional splitting, corruption and reward

Reflections for leaders

- How could your organisation create more opportunities for collaboration?
- What internal or external partnerships have you not thought about?
- What stresses might you be transmitting to your team or at home?
- If you watch yourself and what is going on, like a film – from the outside – what do you see?

Reflections for coaches

- What are the tribes in your organisation?
- What factions have you not noticed?
- What signals do you send – examples of deliberate ones?
- Examples of non-deliberate signals – what was their impact?

Closing thoughts

From these vivid and varied stories, working in the international development aid sector can appear to be at once exciting, inspiring, challenging, exhausting, disillusioning and humbling. The management of staff dealing with trauma and conflict, danger and cultural pressures is immense. It takes a great deal of energy.

For leaders and their staff to function well and to promote both individual and organisational sustainability, leaders must anticipate signs of faltering emotional resilience and physical fatigue as early as possible. The more difficult the terrain and the more challenging the emergency, the more important it is to come to work, consciously alert to one's own emotions and attuned to needs of others. This constant watch applies also when managing staff remotely. In other words, one must look out for signs of burn out even with staff you 'can't see', because they are stationed in various offices and in different countries across a region.

One leader talks of lowering her usually high standards when working in particularly strenuous or traumatic conditions. She asks less of her staff because she has learned to become able as a leader, to accept 'good enough'. Earlier in her career she could not make this adjustment. It is not about a desire for lower quality output, but a realistic and compassionate recalculation which enables the work to continue and the staff to do their best. There are times when it is appropriate even for high performers to slightly lower their expectations.

This strategy aims to prevent burn out, through creating a caring and flexible working atmosphere. It recognises the impact on a person of working in difficult, unpredictable and sometimes emotionally shocking circumstances.

Some non-governmental development organisations schedule rest and relaxation breaks every six weeks. Staff usually go abroad, to escape the restrictions of the compound or office base, to somewhere less dangerous. But the very nature of the work – conflict, a disease outbreak, a refugee influx, the sheer volume of people needing to be helped – often means these breaks are delayed or not taken for many months.

This presents another leadership dilemma. How do you continue to rescue and deliver, whilst maintaining the physical and mental health of your staff? If you are the leader, there is an imperative for good supervision and acute self-monitoring for signs of post-traumatic stress disorder (PTSD) and other indicators that psychological wellbeing is being compromised. But the realities of resourcing staff absences can be a challenge with no immediate practical solution.

It is here that protocols set out neatly and with good intention at the head office can fall flat. Or that local staff refuse to adhere to the rules in the heat of a humanitarian crisis. In such circumstances, passion risks being a primary obstruction to health and resilience. Dedicated staff can become sucked into the very drama they are trying to alleviate. Their managers, feeling the same, may fail to find ways to uphold the R&R protocol either for themselves or for others.

However, it is essential that leaders try to help their staff recognise when they are nearing the edge of their capacity to cope and function well in their job. Insight is needed to spot how events going on outside the team risk playing out *inside* it. I would counsel a revision of what behaviours organisations and colleagues 'reward' – either consciously or unconsciously.

Self-sacrifice in an emergency is one thing. Permanent overstretch, risking illness, burn out or even the development of patterns of abusive behaviour developing are quite another. Such decline ultimately risks organisational reputation, its ability to deliver on its remit and potentially also the ability of it to recruit and retain staff long term. Finding what 'good enough' looks like in such a fraught and pressurised context may be the key to remaining personally and systemically resilient enough to continue the work next week, next month and beyond – when the existential situation may ease up a bit, or not.

Names and organisations have been changed. Examples have been merged and may not represent one single person or organisation.

Notes

1 http://www.undp.org/content/dam/undp/library/corporate/fast-facts/english/FF_CAR_Sept2014.pdf
2 'Rivetted detachment' is a term coined by Liz Macann, former head of coaching at the BBC. By rivetted detachment she means listening, fully present and engaged but able to separate from or not be sucked in by the story.

Chapter 2

A hero is someone who wins a war, not loses a leg

How a Paralympic coach led his diversely disabled athletes to gold

> *My para cyclists have taught me to value every interaction and every conversation. . . . The more I think about people, the better results I achieve.*

Harry shares his reflections on how to achieve elite, world class performance from a collective of diversely disabled athletes. I coached Harry leading up to the Rio 2016 Olympic Games in Brazil. He claims that the executive leadership coaching he received directly impacted his athletes' performance. The paracycling team beat their projected medal targets of 14, achieving 21 medals including 12 gold. Their contribution to a well of national pride was notable. In this chapter Harry explains how, as a senior sports coach, he leads such a team of differently disabled competitors towards outstanding performance targets and beyond target successes. The chapter explores how his para athletes inform Harry's growth as a leader, how they influence his performance and growth. This chapter also explores the concept of diversity within diversity. It also uncovers additional themes, such as reframing disaster or loss, visible injury, inclusivity, parallel process, using self as instrument and choice of attitude (Frankl 1984).

How a Paralympic coach led his diversely disabled athletes to gold

> *I have an ex-military guy who had a leg blown off in a war, a young woman born without an arm and another who injured her back in an industrial accident. Four of my athletes are partially sighted, one has multiple sclerosis and several others are on heavy drug regimes, to manage their illness or to cope with constant pain.*

Harry leads an exceptionally diverse team. A collective of global, elite, high performance, disabled athletes. Each member of the team has different physiological and psychological needs. Harry's job is to work out how to lead them to optimal performance, competing in the European and World Championships, as well as at the Olympic Games. This is about points, medals and sponsorship deals. It's about winning:

> *As a leader of a Paralympic team, I have a range of approaches in my head. Normally, Olympians must fit into the system that everybody else is working in. But with my para athletes, I do it the other way around: I mould the system around my athletes' attitudes and beliefs. You create such a powerful organisation, when each athlete is working hard in training, because their motivation is about them and what they can do about the results they're aiming for.*

'Para' as in the Paralympic games, comes from the ancient Greek meaning 'alongside' or parallel (Lacey and Mounter 2012). Holding the Paralympic competition two weeks after the 'main' Olympic Games doesn't seem to honour the notion of alongside. It feels the opposite of parity. In my view both competitions should be held simultaneously, however logistically intense this may be for the host city.

Visible injury and mental resilience

Harry's athletes contend with physical and emotional challenges throughout the day, nearly every day. One of the most striking things he says he observes is the difference in choice of attitude (Frankl 1984) between his para sportsmen and women. Each of them greets their handicap differently. Let's take the former solider, injured in Afghanistan:

> *Ex-military people are conditioned to thinking of themselves as a number in a system. They're used to rules in a structured, organised environment. They're not used to owning their own thinking. In their world, you're not there to think, you're there to do a job.*
>
> *When a soldier loses a leg, they lose their career, their regiment, their buddies; they lose the whole structure of working and living alongside their colleagues and friends. Whilst dealing with being tragically injured, they're simultaneously coping with losing their identity – their future.*

Some of this injury or hurt is visible, but some is not. The culture of the military creates psychological mechanisms for 'dealing with' tragedy or loss. For example, if a soldier is badly injured and can't go into battle again, he or she may be given 'hero' status. With the loss of one identity, the system provides another. But who is this for? It is assumed it is to help the injured soldier who's just seen their career collapse. Hero status may help avoid going into victim mode, associated with attack and feelings of redundancy. It may also offer a convenient device for fit soldiers to avoid the emotional pain their injured colleague is causing *them* to experience. Hero status for the fallen may enable serving soldiers to return to the theatre of war and carry on with the job.

The shock of what's happened can be devastating physically and emotionally. Soldiers don't feel like heroes at all. Some may even feel survivor guilt if a colleague dies or is more severely injured than they are.

As the injured try to recover and adjust, they must relearn how to move and how to interact with other people. Their trauma is not just physical. A missing limb is easily identified. People can talk about it. The injury or loss is recognisable. But psychological injury, such as PTSD – post-traumatic stress disorder – can be like an invisible wound. Such damage is harder to illustrate. People do not talk about it or do not know *how* to talk about it. Ex-servicemen may not know they are suffering from post-traumatic stress disorder. Some refuse to acknowledge it, for psychological injury may increase feelings of impotence created by physical wounds.

A hero is someone who wins a war, not loses a leg. Yet hero status is a way of honouring great sacrifice and bravery in service of the nation. Or a way for the military to move a person out of the organisation that has held their identity and achievement until now. It is a way of avoiding shame or a sense of failure.

Hero status may be a useful device for dealing with transition (i.e. leaving the military) whilst an injured soldier establishes their new focus and purpose in life. In the case of Paralympians, the transition from winning one kind of medal for elite performance to winning another kind of medal, this time for sporting excellence, offers a bridge between the old and the new high-performance environment.

From the theatre of war to Broadway

Harry has a former lighting technician in his team. She fell off a ladder at work and damaged the top five vertebrae in her back. This industrial accident was hugely traumatic. She went from being an active, capable professional who was part of major theatre productions, to sitting in a wheelchair for two years. She now works as a physiotherapist, cycling around the city with crutches strapped to her bike. The saddle and handlebars take the weight so her legs don't have to. She cannot walk, but she can ride.

It took a couple of years for this former theatre professional to reimagine her working life. She tried para winter sports and para rock climbing but found cycling suited her best. She now combines two new careers – one caring career as a physiotherapist and one competitive career as a para cyclist. This athlete appears to be successfully reconciling the can-can't tug of all that she is no longer able to do, with the imperative to train, perform and be fit for what she *is able* to do.

Harry's job is to manage his team's varied and simultaneous, different needs towards competitive success. As a leader, Harry consciously puts the para athlete at the centre of their own story:

> *It's about finding out what you are good at and seeing how that can work for you. . . . All my athletes have a choice of reaction to their situation. They'll work out what they can do with two legs but only one arm. Another athlete will have both arms, but one leg missing. Some have all their limbs but can't see.*

For the former theatre technician, the nature of the performance appears to have changed, as has the nature of the stage. This individual has made a radical transition from shining the spotlight on others to being the one in the spotlight. She's transitioned from residing in the shadows, working up a ladder on a lighting rig, to being highly visible and exposed, with the sporting arena as her stage.

Leading people in pain

During Harry's coaching sessions, we worked through the emotional impact on him of what he sees his athletes contend with. He describes the multiple responses to loss and endings he has witnessed:

> *One person's response is to feel as if they're the same as everybody else and get on with it. Whilst another person is permanently resentful, playing the victim and expecting people to wrap them in cotton wool, to cosset them and protect them. In other cases, it can be the parents who set up a 'victim' pattern of thinking in their child. Some athletes have learned to 'play' their disability. They carry the 'I'm different' card and expect to be treated differently from everyone else.*

I ask Harry about the impact on him as a sports coach, of leading athletes who want to stay stuck in victimhood. Does Harry absorb the resentment? Or do his athletes absorb his? Is Harry at risk of inhabiting a victim stance too, in the sense of having to lead such 'difficult' people? Harry faces the dilemma of whether to express or mask his frustration. The para athlete is bound to pick up on this, consciously or subconsciously. The dynamic of transferred emotions is likely to impact other members of the team too.

I hypothesise that taking up a victim stance represents how the parents of a disabled child sometimes feel; might they be projecting their own feelings of envy or hardship connected to bringing up a disabled child, compared to peers who gave birth to able-bodied children – peers whom they assume 'have it easy'? The competitive success they desire for their child could be a transference of their own competitive feelings of winning or losing in life.

Harry acknowledges the challenges of coping with ordinary life, for someone born with or adjusting to a disability. His humility is clear to see:

> *I regularly try to imagine what it's like being in their shoes [sic, or shoe]. How many of us take for granted our first day at school? Or making friends in the playground. Imagine turning up on your first day in a new school, with a prosthetic leg? The other kids looking at it, calling you nicknames, not being able to join in with stuff. Added to that is the sheer effort of getting to or around school, on crutches or with a white stick.*

Breakdown as a breakthrough

In the lead up to the Rio Olympic Games in 2016, Harry fell off his mountain bike. He broke his wrist. At the time, his children were one and two and a half years old. Harry went from an admired professional, provider and capable co-parent to not being able to do up his own shoe laces or change a diaper. Consider Harry's now own infantilised position. He had to ask for help getting to work. When he arrived, he had to ask for help, opening the door.

The break turned out to be complex. Two operations followed. As his coach, I saw Harry's sudden, albeit temporary, disability as potentially ripe territory to explore parallel process: Understanding disability. Understanding his athletes. Further understanding himself. A parallel process is spotting where something is happening in one area of life, which may echo something individual or organisational going on in another. In Harry's case, having an arm out of action mirrors the experience of some of his athletes who are forced to manage without a limb:

> *Breaking my wrist was a small, insignificant way of experiencing the whole picture of what it is to be disabled. Every task takes twice as long. You're busy thinking all day. You're making adjustments. Like putting the phone in the other pocket; I kept missing calls, searching for the phone with the wrong arm or in the pocket I couldn't reach.*

Not surprisingly perhaps, Harry grew a beard because he couldn't shave left handed. Showering took ages, as he struggled to keep the plastered arm dry by wrapping it in a plastic bag. Those may not sound like big things, but they generated stress. It is important to consider the impact on performance when multiple stressors are layered up throughout the day on top of everything else. Harry found the coaching we did during his recovery unexpected and enriching. He now adjusts his expectations of athletes:

> *If I'd been an athlete, I'd have felt so stressed some days I wouldn't be ready for a new input on how to train, or to up my performance target. One training*

session in a day may not look particularly challenging, but the cognitive load of getting out of the house, on and off the train and a tram to reach the track venue can feel like a days' work in itself. By the time some of my athletes arrive at the track, they can't train well. Their tank is empty.

I think it is also worth reflecting on the energy required to ask for help. This is the internal dilemma of whether to keep trying, and for how long, or whether to ask for help straight away. Asking can feel like giving in. It was another new experience for Harry.

Consider also the energy it takes people – particularly those who tend towards introversion – to externalise instead of internalising as they might normally, each thought, need, action and intention. Imagine playing 'see-it-say-it' all day. This energetic demand uses up precious physical and emotional capacity which would otherwise be channelled into winning a race.

The invitation to see a setback, trauma or breakdown as a *breakthrough* is a concept leaders and coaches can make good use of in their reflective practice (Bion 1962). Harry's broken wrist represents a 'break' or a rest from the continuum. It forced him to stop. It forced him to take heavy painkillers. It forced him to confront disability, albeit temporarily.

The fracture might also have offered him a break from the 'strain' of being able bodied amidst a sea of disabled colleagues. A break from able-bodied guilt. The break represents a release from constantly empathising with others and instead indulging in the stress and frustration of disability first hand. The break may be the first time that Harry is truly able to join his team, in a metaphorical sense. It offers him the opportunity to analyse whether a fundamental rethink or change is necessary e.g. to the skeletal structure of the team or the organization. One could extend the metaphor and view the joints of the body as junctions or choice points or an opportunity to take a different path.

Harry's injury had the potential to create greater closeness or empathy, between him and his athletes. Conversely, it might accentuate an emotional disconnect because he will recover, and they will not. Harry was embarrassed when he found himself moaning about being so hampered to one of his para athletes:

I talked to one of my guys who'd lost his arm and some of his calves through a shrapnel injury. I was complaining about my arm and everything I couldn't manage to do. Then I looked up. We smiled at each other. I felt like such an idiot. But this ex-soldier said it was refreshing for him to hear what he'd felt too.

So, voicing the hurt, the pain, the frustration and stress can be acceptable – even if it's from someone travelling through a setback, not staying in it for good. This includes when the scale of injury or damage is incomparable.

The evolving leader

Harry is changing his leadership style through working with para athletes:

> *As I can't guess what it's like to not be able to see properly, or to lose a limb, I ask my athletes to describe it to me. And then to describe what race they want to do, what time they want as their target and how they want to achieve it.*

These are classic coaching techniques, starting with offering high quality of listening, empathy and presence – asking about goals, options and actions. Harry then follows this up by offering the athlete control. Ownership. A self-empowerment approach. Harry did some of this intuitively. But he also consciously learned to employ the ingredients of a coaching conversation:

> *I believe, the more you can focus on the other person, the better job you'll be able to do for them. I've made a transition as a leader. In my younger coaching days, I used to tell people what I know, how they could improve and how hard they'd need to work to get there. But in the last couple of years, I've switched [my] approach. What drives me now is to think how they're motivated, to ask them where they want to go. It's turned from instruction to question.*

Harry evidences an increasingly person-centred approach and has shifted from a directive, towards a non-directive, coaching approach to leadership. This is congruent with a self-empowerment perspective. His team is packed with people who've reimagined their lives and their potential in response to disability at birth or through accident, trauma or aggressive injury. The diversity of trauma is notable. And the diverse way Harry approaches leading his team offers exceptional insights and learning for the rest of us. For a start, he doesn't call his group of cyclists a team. He calls them a 'collective'. That's because of the eclectic mix of people who, had circumstances been different, may never have ended up in competitive sport at all, let alone the same team. Their targets and goals are not uniform. Their motivations have different roots. Yet everyone is heading towards optimal performance and success, as *they* define it. There is no imposition of homogeneity, which I think means everyone retains their individual identity in a way that embraces diversity.

> *People assume it's all about winning medals. That everyone is doing the same sport with the same aim. But for my para athletes, competing can be more about validating them as people. Some are competing for themselves. Others are racing for someone else.*

Harry must produce medal winning performances from his Paralympians. After all, that is the formal measure of success in his job. The thrill of competing for his athletes is insufficient without a gold, silver or bronze to accompany it. As we know, winning medals attracts funding and sponsorship. Athletes not going for gold won't be picked for the squad.

In order to achieve outstanding race times and medals success, Harry advanced as a person and developed his leadership style. His focus has shifted from a hunger to achieve the end point to, instead, forging a holistic understanding of each athlete's origins, life experiences and potential.

Diversity within diversity

Another para athlete is racing, following a stroke. Before every race, she looks at a picture of a stroke victim she is racing for. She competes for everyone who has had a stroke. For her it is about what you can get out of life after a stroke. Standing on a podium wearing a medal represents having a choice about what you do and how you do it. Or deciding that you do indeed have choice. One of her teammates is a former able-bodied track and field athlete who developed multiple sclerosis:

> *On the approach to a race, we construct a warm up to switch her muscles on, to fire everything up. Her performance was totally mind-blowing and amazing. After the race we have to lift her off her bike, with her muscles still twitching and kicking. . . . Her muscles keep firing for hours after the race. . . . It's totally exhausting so she'll sleep 15 hours the night after a race. We use this particular warm up very rarely as it's so stressful and fatiguing.*

Harry knows he has a serious duty of care towards the wellbeing of such athletes:

> *There's the insightful preparation and the conversation you have with a competitor before the race. They have complete faith in you because it'll get them what they want, which is to win that race. They know the impact that a race has on their body will compromise what they look like on TV. If you're prepared to sacrifice all that to win the event, then it's a privilege to know people prepared to commit to your leadership on that level.*

Harry shares another poignant anecdote concerning the four partially sighted cyclists in his team. Each have different levels of sight and light sensitivity. One has a guide dog, another a white stick. Each needs bespoke logistical support. This includes making the lights brighter for one but reducing their glare for another. Partially sighted cyclists also need somebody sighted to ride with. So, part of Harry's job is leading and motivating tandem riders, not just his para cyclist. The issue of dependency is yet another issue Harry must help his partially sighted cyclists navigate:

> *Para cyclists need to tell their tandem rider what they're aiming for. People will want to connect with your goal and help you. Tough as this may sound,*

asking for help is part of the deal, like being short. . . . You'll always have to ask people to reach the top shelf in the supermarket for you! If you're not comfortable asking for help, you should pick a different job – a different goal – like gardening or IT.

For the first time during my conversation with Harry, a harshness seeps through his normally warm and enthusiastic tone of voice. Employing the concept of 'self as instrument', I regularly ask Harry about this, curious about how his job and the people he leads, makes him feel. I now do similarly, noticing how the harshness in Harry's voice affects me. It felt 'tough'. Maybe 'tough' represents how tough life can feel for Harry's para athletes. Perhaps it represents how at times Harry finds it tough to lead people dealt such a challenge at birth or later in life. He may have developed his own tough exterior (or is it interior) in order to cope with his own version of survivor's guilt. Again, we consider the suffering of those encountering another's difficult circumstances. As a leader Harry must 'hold' or contain occasional aggression from, or aggressively challenging pain experienced by, his athletes. He must make sure not to absorb too much of it, lest he compromise his own wellbeing and ability to lead.

Whether through injury, disease or disability at birth, managing a collective of para athletes is an intense job. It carries logistical and emotional complexity. I am in no doubt about how privileged and rewarded Harry feels:

We have lovely quiet chats with riders after races, they'll say they never thought they were capable of doing this or that. It fuels you to challenge and stretch. You look back at all the tough conversations about not being good enough. And I think you can never have enough difficult conversations if the outcomes are that good.

Transport, sneezes and community

High performance sports events are like ripe immunology centres, full of fit, pumped up athletes from all over the world, exchanging germs. So, risk, exposure and protection from disease is another consideration for an Olympic team leader, whose charges may have reduced immunity because of illness or medication regimes.

The concept of the Olympic Village is about togetherness. Some country's teams spend hours socialising in the canteen. It is an opportunity of a lifetime! But whilst one culture might be highly resilient to certain strains of coughs and sneezes, another is not. Harry does not want his athletes to catch a bug that will wreck their race.

There are so many different health elements to manage, in order to optimise performance at the Games. As well as managing nutrition and muscle performance, Harry also helps his athletes manage pain. He observes that personality, upbringing and choice of attitude influence how an individual perceives and judges pain. For one Paralympian, pain is a positive indicator, but for most it feels harmful, alarming or stressful:

> *If an athlete's taking drugs to manage pain and tiredness, it becomes like a different currency. . . . One athlete with a tumour on his spine, regards pain as a feedback mechanism. Feedback that's he's alive and functioning. When he describes pain in his leg, he says he feels excited, that everything's firing and his muscles are working. That's an amazing feeling for him. For others it's the body's way of telling them to be careful and manage themselves appropriately.*

Harry's conscious use of 'choice of attitude', is a strategy to give the athlete back some degree of control. Control is well known as an antidote to stress, both for the able bodied and the disabled. Harry discusses pain with his athletes, asking them how hard they want to push themselves in a training session. Sometimes his athletes decide to hold back on training hard and deep, in order not to limit their performance in a race. On other days, they recalibrate what painful is for them.

In addition to managing diverse disability and causes of disability, Harry also manages diverse mental attitudes towards disability. With different training schedules, targets and underpinning motivations to race, it is a constant juggle of the psychological and the practical.

When it comes to the logistics of flying a team across the world to the Olympic Games, Harry rehearses lots of 'what if' scenarios with the athletes; for example, travel arrangements going wrong, injury, illness and jetlag. The impact of travelling varies widely. Many of the athletes are good at sport, but not well travelled. Even though they're a determined bunch of people, the unexpected during transit can overwhelm them:

> *You can easily do two hours of walking in the airport on a travel day, without realising it. That can tire a para athlete. But they don't want to sit in a wheelchair. I understand why. We must remember the social perception of being in a wheelchair. Some airports insist official airport staff push you. People don't want that either. But if it's pitched and discussed in the right way, we can manage the situation successfully.*

We can see how Harry and his extended team of physiotherapists, medics, nutritionists and logistics managers must develop a suite of influencing and persuading skills, quite apart from their specialist knowledge of sport. The focus is on remaining calm and on finding solutions. Harry does not want his athletes' energy wasted through upset and stress:

> *For example, a visually impaired athlete may wear dark glasses, so their exposure to light and dark i.e., whether it's daytime or night time, won't happen as it does for the rest of us.*

Flying them halfway around the world means allowing more time for them to adjust to a new time zone. The training schedule reflects this. It's a similar story with the athletes' eating regime.

Medication adds yet more facets to consider, not just from a health perspective but also from a compliance and doping point of view. The athletes travel with lots of painkillers which help to keep them mobile during the journey. Prescription drugs must be taken at the right times. Some athletes need up to 12 prescription drugs to be able to function. Each drug they take must be listed. Even protein shakes must be logged so the drug testers know what might show up. Compare this level of medication with an able-bodied athlete who may have taken a paracetamol tablet two days earlier.

With so much preparation and forethought just to arrive at a competition event, it's hardly surprising that para athletes are often seen relishing just being at the Games. But Harry insists the Paralympic Games is not a 'participation event' as some people perceive them, but most definitely a competition. Harry believes that Paralympians have a different psychology compared to able-bodied athletes:

> *They're aware of how fragile life can be. How what you have can all be taken away tomorrow. These athletes stand out because they are full of appreciation for other people's journey, not just their own.*

Both para- and able-bodied athletes are clearly here to win. But sometimes the world's greatest able-bodied sportsmen and women aren't necessarily the most emotionally resilient. Harry explains:

> *Able-bodied athletes are very physically gifted, normal people. They've often done well at school and been picked out as talented individuals. There's no doubt about it, an Olympian's life is tough. It demands sacrifices and compromise. There they are at the Olympic Games and nothing's gone wrong yet. These elite athletes usually haven't been exposed to a colossal life experience, trauma or loss.*

As a result, Harry believes the range of what upsets an able-bodied athlete can be narrower than for a para athlete. Not coming first, or not being selected for a race, can devastate an able-bodied competitor. Harry explains:

> *Compare that to people with a bigger range of experience, where the outcome has been that they've lost an arm . . . well, coming second not first, may affect them in no way whatsoever.*

Closing thoughts

Through working with disabled athletes, Harry has developed an understanding of multiple forms of and routes to disability. He has learned how to lead when there is injury, disease or a complex medical regime to follow. He leads with empowering conversations, questions, empathy and individual focused approaches.

Harry seeks to listen and learn. He has clear goal-based parameters in his job as coach to the paracycling team. Within some narrow and obvious aims – winning medals – Harry demonstrates impressive and dexterous leadership capability. The diversity, complexity and combination of simultaneous physical and psychological considerations of his athletes is a considerable challenge. Harry helps people understand and handle their choices and the consequences that follow.

The variety of experiences and exposure to other people's stories and circumstances associated with Harry's job seems exceptional. Look at the diversity within diversity involved in the various causes and types of disability.

I prompt able-bodied athletes, some of whom are arguably the strongest, fastest and most disciplined elite sportsmen and women in the world, to reflect on any external or internal handicaps they may hold. Leaders in other fields of work can do the same, to consider what we can learn from para athletes about resilience, mastery and recovery from trauma or failure.

Having digested the previous Olympic Games in Rio de Janeiro, Harry heads to Tokyo with the next Olympic cycle in mind: Japan 2020:

> *Rio was a journey for the athletes, but it was a journey for me as well. For the next Olympic Games, it's important not to repeat the same journey. I need to stay authentic, and make sure Japan is challenging. I know it sounds selfish, but it needs to be a stretch for me, to create a stretch for others.*

Harry explains more about his internal mindset for ongoing success:

> *I decide what I need out of a competition, to be fuelled to create a pathway for everyone else in the team. I can delegate elements of planning and strategy. But to create a bigger leadership impact in Tokyo, there's more I can do by creating more time, a clearer mission about what I want us to achieve and how I want to achieve it. With Rio I worked it out along the way – the feel, the pace, the pressure. But I could have made this clearer from the outset.*

Harry says he sets out to learn first and lead next. Goals and measurable outcomes are thought through together with his athletes. It's a co-created, experimental and emergent approach. His ambition is to help his athletes achieve more than they thought they could:

> *Leading para athletes has taught me to value every interaction and every conversation. It's about the importance of the other person. The more I do that, the better I can coach them. There are radically different levels of what hard work looks like for one person, compared to for another. But I am mindful to balance how hard I push my athletes, with not losing their trust.*

As well as thinking about what leading a para athlete team may have taught Harry about leadership, I ask what this courageous collection of hugely diverse individuals has taught him, about himself:

> *Whether you view the glass as half empty, or half full, you have a choice. There's always someone out there in a worse situation than you, who's handling it better than you. For me, the para athlete context is so utterly life affirming . . .*
>
> *Seeing these athletes' approach to life, their ability to see sport as an opportunity, an adventure, a journey, gives me real confidence that if something changed dramatically in my life – if I had to move house, if I lost my job, if something significantly difficult happened in my life – that I'd be very OK with it. It could be something traumatic and life changing . . . but I've had the privilege to know people who've had huge situations and dealt with them.*

A hero is someone who wins a war, not loses a leg: how a Paralympic coach led his diversely disabled athletes to gold

Reflections for leaders

- What types of disability – physical, mental or metaphorical – do you manage in your work environment?
- Who are the 'able bodied' in your organisation?
- Who are the heroes?
- Where/when can loss of identity be experienced?
- When could you have employed 'choice of attitude' (Frankl 1984) as a concept?
- Where is the spotlight in your organisation?
- Who or what is it shining on?
- Which individuals are or what part of the organisation is operating in the shadows?
- Where is there pain in your organisation?
- Using self as instrument – when do you notice how your employee/s make you feel? May this represent something about *their feelings rather than yours?*

Reflections for coaches

- Considering disability within oneself – both visible and invisible
- Where is there visible stress?
- Where might there be stress that can't be illustrated?
- Combining caring with competitive
- Where is there pain for you the leader?

- What issues are not being dealt with, because people can't see them or don't want to see them?
- What identity is provided for this leader by their system?
- Where is there pain for this organisation?

References

Bion, W. (1962). *Learning From Experience*. Oxford: Rowman and Littlefield.

Frankl, V. (1984). *Man's Search for Meaning: An Introduction to Logotherapy*. New York: Touchstone (p. 75).

Lacey, M. and Mounter, P. (2012). *The Story of the Olympics*. London. Usborne Publishing.

Chapter 3

Stocking the World Foods aisle

The story of how a global supermarket manager had to relearn how to lead effectively, in a multi-ethnic context

> *I order 200 tonnes of yellow mangoes a week; but if the pesticide residue levels are too high for European legal requirements, we can't import any of them. Stuff arrives off the ship in big brown boxes, which are totally unsuitable to display in-store. Unpacking and restacking the shelves adds staff time and process. As a result, we have to charge the customer more.*

This leader works at a global supermarket chain. She is based in the UK, stocking 200 stores with foods desired by lower income customers and an influx of middle class shoppers who want to reduce their weekly spending. Our leader is an experienced buyer. When she was asked to head up the World Foods aisle, she was delighted, but subsequently found she was failing to lead her team effectively and that her ability to connect with suppliers had stalled.

This is the story of a former coaching client who, seeing my international and multi-cultural experience, approached me to help her relearn how to lead. Together we explored how she went about building the right relationships across and outside her team. We examined her underused personal narrative for its potential to create greater human connection with others. And we discussed how this leader invests in understanding her customers better, before doing business. She is now making an unexpected impact on the broader business.

Stocking the World Foods aisle: the story of how a global supermarket manager had to relearn how to lead effectively, in a multi-ethnic context

> *It's a fun category. Better than my previous job buying nuts and crisps! There's so much to learn, when you're dealing with a 20-part supply chain of rice growers, pickers, packers, pallet movers and shippers . . all speaking different languages, sending food across the globe. Then there are the middle men. And the factories and distributors here in the UK. Most are multi-generation family concerns, all in the business of filling our cupboards with exotic produce.*

My client, a recently promoted leader in a global supermarket chain, reflects on the complexity of her role. She finds managing a multi-cultural team of negotiators, cutting deals across 35 different nationalities and markets, stimulating, humbling and sometimes highly challenging. Antonia had to relearn how to lead in what was a changeable and, for her, new context.

In her old job, Antonia took logistics for granted. There was certainty. She knew how international business worked. Orders took two days. Palates were a standard size. Goods were a consistent weight and quality. Everything arrived pre-packaged to fit exactly onto the supermarket shelf – not so in ethnic foods!

It cannot be assumed that an order of 200 palates of yams or a shipment of chapati flour will be the same size as the previous order. The buying team is dealing with small plot farmers. The quality of what they produce varies. On a typical order of 200 tonnes of yellow mangoes a week, for example, if pesticide residue levels are too high for European legal requirements, the supermarket cannot import them. Other foodstuffs arrive in big brown boxes, which are totally unsuitable to display in-store. Unpacking and restacking the shelves adds staff time and process. As a result, the supermarket must charge the customer more.

Instead of orders taking two days, as they do in nuts and crisps, it can take three weeks to move a tonne of garam masala spice, or a consignment of salted fish from its source, to a supermarket in the UK. There are other concerns too, such as cultural sensitivities, political instability in the country of origin, shipping conditions or freak weather events. Tsunamis and hurricanes can stop a ship leaving port for weeks. Orders fall behind; there are early rains, late rains or no rains at all. That can mean failed harvests, a supply shortage and rising prices. This dynamic and exciting category requires resilience, forethought and planning.

To shepherd a team, and upwards manage the Board in such inconsistent and unpredictable circumstances, a leader needs to be able to manage ambiguity and last-minute change. Employees must be able to adapt at short notice and to think resourcefully. If they cannot, one supermarket will be out of stock whilst its competitors are happily trading away.

The excitement yet unpredictability of the ethnic foods category creates a compelling business case for supermarkets and independent shops struggling to hang on to healthy profits.

The business case for ethnic foods

This is a particularly complicated part of supermarket trading. It is also an area of the retail sector offering exponential growth. One international supermarket estimates that its ethnic food category is growing by 34%, year on year. Many parts of the FMCG [fast moving consumer goods] market are battling with negative growth. That means that they are still making a profit, but every year that profit is going down. In contrast, the ethnic foods market is expanding rapidly.

Britain's multi-cultural communities now make up 13% of the population.[1] Many so-called 'ethnic' shoppers are British-born descendants of immigrant parents or grandparents who identify strongly with their family origins and cuisine. They tend to have bigger families, and they cook from scratch and enjoy their meals, eating together. They entertain more. Even low-income families from ethnic backgrounds typically prefer to prepare fresh meals, rather than buying ready meals, even if, as is often the case, packet meals are cheaper.

So, this is a story about the role that food plays in different cultures, as well as an economically exciting opportunity. A standard white British customer's basket spending is £23 per week. A family of Caribbean, Middle Eastern, African or Asian origin spends twice that. Even families on modest budgets are more generous when it comes to spending on food. All the more so when there is a special occasion like Eid, Diwali, a wedding party or Jewish new year.

Ethnic spending is a significant opportunity for all the supermarkets. The market in specialist foods in the UK grew by 24% between 2007 and 2011 (Mintel Survey 2012). It is expected to continue to grow by 6% per year (Mintel Survey 2012), representing a leap from a £1.8 billion proposition in 2007 (*The Guardian* 2007) to an estimated £5.14 billion by 2020.

And it's not just food. There is potential for other areas of the retail sector to expand as well. For example, Asian families use huge cooking pots to prepare meals for an extended family. Caribbean women need big bra sizes and 'nude' tights that look good on brown skin. Indian and Middle Eastern families buy red and pink occasion wear for festivals or wedding parties. These customers are looking for specific products which appropriately reflect their ethnic heritage, culture or religious customs.

The discerning ethnic shopper

Antonia defines an ethnic food as a product from a community's home country, for example, basmati rice, salami, salted fish, ghee or gherkins:

> *Dolmio tomato sauce is not an ethnic food. It's a brand, designed to look and feel Italian. But it isn't Italian. The ethnic customer wants to buy authentic, quality food from brands they trust.*

When a brand of Polish gherkins did not sell, Antonia wanted to find out why. It turned out the gherkins weren't Polish at all . . . but an invented 'Pol-*ish*' brand of cucumbers which were picked, pickled and packaged in Britain. The Polish community saw through it. Antonia had no idea.

There was another lesson for the buying team during Diwali when some Hindu customers refused to buy rice with a Pakistani flag on the packet. There are Pakistani customers who avoid Indian rice. They may claim the taste is different. Whether it is the flavour, patriotism or political tensions between nations playing out in the supermarket aisle, the ethnic foods buying team must learn fast from its mistakes, to prevent commercial loss and not alienate these highly valued customers.

Leaders in a global marketplace must cultivate an awareness of diversity within diversity. Cypriot families prefer a different brand of cous cous to Turks; Greeks prefer a different make of vine leaves compared to Lebanese customers. At Ramadan, West African Muslims eat fish, Turkish Muslims cook lamb and Asian Muslims choose chicken for their celebratory meals in the evenings. The buying team must be sensitive to this and carry deep cultural knowledge to anticipate their customers' simultaneous and differing needs. My client needed to develop an awareness of these nuanced requirements and reframe her buying practices. She also needed to manage the risk of perceived favouritism within her nascent team.

Building the right buying team, then listening to it

At the time of her appointment, this supermarket's ethnic foods team was all white, female and British. A year later, it was staffed by a young, male Wahabi Muslim from Saudi Arabia, another Indian man and an older African Hindu of Indian extraction; there was a female Polish buyer and a Jamaican. Having created a more globally representative team, Antonia decided to change the name of the ethnic foods division:

> *My team told me that using the term 'ethnic' was culturally insensitive. As if there is something wrong with you if you're from an ethnic minority. They felt 'World Foods' was better. So that's now what we're now called.*

The team continued to grow. A new female Indian buyer joined. She was tasked with negotiating Jamaican and Oriental goods. Antonia wanted to foster more cultural cross-overs, building the intra-cultural and inter-cultural knowledge of her buyers to increase the flexibility of her team. (I think this was ambitious but worth attempting.) Success may pivot on whether members of the team can up-skill each other and facilitate successful supplier relationships for each other. Antonia used the coaching space to explore issues of rivalry and competitiveness within her team.

The learning leader

Antonia was prepared to re-examine her leadership style including changing how she leads, in order to succeed in a multi-ethnic context. She felt on a number of fronts that she was failing, after previously being seen as a successful manager of people, product and logistics.

Antonia kept wondering why her highly knowledgeable buyers didn't think for themselves. She realised how much of the time in a conversation she spent 'telling' rather than 'asking'. She was constantly solving. In some cultures, it is expected that the boss will tell you what to do. There is an additional complication when a junior male employee finds he is being told what to do by an assertive, more senior female manager.

Through asking, listening and softening her tone of voice, Antonia's team gradually became more receptive to her leadership, evidencing more creativity, confidence and independent thinking. They shifted into being in the 'adult' mode [as opposed to 'child' or 'helpless' modes] (Berne 1973). Her buyers moved out of a passive state and began to take the initiative. Antonia says she is now coaching rather than directing.

In another culturally driven anecdote, the mother of one of Antonia's buyers rang her on her mobile phone. She told Antonia how worried she was about her son's stress levels because of work. His mother asked Antonia to look after him: '*Please could you not shout at him?*', she asked. Antonia heard how this employee was fairly new to the country and as the sole male in the family was the provider, looking after his parents as well as his wife and child.

At first Antonia couldn't understand why her staff member was so offended. After all, her leadership style had worked in other teams. Indeed, people had always wanted to work for her:

> *Leading such an ethnically diverse team, I started to appreciate that you need to treat people how they want to be treated. My old ways in nuts & crisps weren't working. That buyer respected me because I'm the boss, but if I criticise him, he feels he's failing me. I have to be aware of this.*

She had to find different ways to lead effectively. To hone her flexibility and range of different leadership approaches, to enable herself and others to perform at their best.

Antonia also realised she needed to work on her supplier relationships. When she arrived in the job, suppliers wouldn't speak to her. They would negotiate with her more junior colleague, a man with less experience. If she visited a Pakistani family-owned factory in the UK, Antonia dressed modestly. But something was wrong. She could not understand it. They just would not do business with her.

Even though Antonia held the keys to £110 million worth of orders for more than 200 supermarkets, it was she who had to adapt her style of doing business to fit in with the culture of her supplier. She was willing to be humble. To try new approaches. Again, as with her team, to seek to understand first, then act. She recognised that it was all about relationships. Antonia was open to learning from her team:

> *My team have educated me. They tell me what to do and what not to do. Not to wear a dress if it's a Muslim supplier, but rather trousers and a long top*

> *and jacket. I've learned what to do to make my suppliers feel respected. To invest time listening, asking about my supplier's family, resisting the urge to rush in to do business the way we expect to in the West.*

Even though she, the client, *is* in *the West*.

Antonia took time to reflect, to seek to understand her supplier's businesses. She thanked them for inviting her to their factory, or for coming to a suppliers conference. Antonia allowed plenty of time for them to talk first – only then did she begin a negotiation.

The difference in results was almost immediate. Antonia became sought after by suppliers, eager to sell their spices, Thai fish sauce, par-boiled rice and patties through her. Greeted with open handshakes and smiles, Antonia is invited to factories and warehouses, to family businesses and special occasions within the business year, like Diwali – which is seen by Hindus as an auspicious time to cut a deal. At a recent suppliers' conference, a queue of male suppliers stood for more than an hour, waiting to speak to Antonia. This time they appeared to ignore many of Antonia's male colleagues. Evidently something had shifted.

The leaders' narrative

Whilst trying to master her new brief in World Foods, Antonia ignored the potential gift of her own family story. One of three children, brought up in Glasgow, she had never bothered to find out about her Italian immigrant roots, until now. Her surname means a hat or cap – igniting for me a series of metaphors around being at the head of something, understanding other people's head-stuff, their thinking, their identity; wondering which 'hat' World Foods customers feel they are wearing – immigrant, descendant, foreigner, ethnic, British, Bangladeshi or Polish Catholic?

Ignoring or not being conscious of her own narrative may have limited Antonia's impact as a business woman in a multi-cultural context. Her invariably male suppliers assumed she was a white, British female. Something apart from them, emphasising difference. Antonia was missing out on the potential to narrow that gap and build a warmth of rapport with her team, her team's families and her suppliers.

Antonia now deliberately leverages her family story. She is learning Italian and using her personal background to deepen professional relationships through mutual respect. It appears to be working. She is cutting deals that weren't possible before. The bottom line is shifting. Narrative is helping Antonia increase her influence and reduce feelings of difference.

Closing thoughts

Antonia's team asked to change the name of the department from 'Ethnic Foods' to 'World Foods'. Staff felt that it brought the customer closer to the brand. The term 'ethnic' felt pejorative to some employees.

From a European or North American perspective, one's idea of a 'world food' may be pomegranate molasses or curry powder. But if you are living in Indonesia or China, a sought after 'ethnic food' may be cheddar cheese, baked beans or Scottish oatcakes. The same is true in Singapore or Russia, where French champagne, Italian parmesan cheese or Yorkshire tea are sought after luxuries. These foods can be perceived as regional specialties or everyday essentials. Different cultures value different foods of course. Not everything is to everyone's taste. But at play here is the desire for the tingling diversity of experience on the taste buds, a nostalgia for 'home' or family origin, a nod to geopolitics and, above all, a call for authenticity that can be trusted.

World Foods continues to evolve and expand as a supermarket category. The team is introducing new food offerings from West Africa e.g., plantains, 90% peanut butter and bigger pack sizes for large families. For the growing Sri Lankan community, there is red rice, salt fish, noodles and stronger spices. Antonia says there's more work to be done on improving the product ranges from China, Thailand and Korea – markets with potential that has been mostly ignored due to lack of expert knowledge.

With such rapid growth and juicy profits, the World Foods category might logically argue its way into becoming the core business of British-based supermarkets. Antonia believes there is still much to learn about where to source and what customers want. She wants to stretch her team even further, broadening their knowledge, experience and flexibility. She wants more cultural cross-overs, with the Polish foods buyer learning to negotiate with Asian spice suppliers and the Caribbean expert having a go at buying cous cous from the Middle East.

The visible success of this team, both with its customers and in terms of the bottom line for the business, is spreading. . . . Buyers from areas of the business which are in negative growth are ringing up the buyers in the World Foods team. They are eager to learn from them. They see the team's motivation, high energy, ideas. . . . They notice buyers in World Foods are out in stores and talking to suppliers instead of agonising over goods-tracking spreadsheets.

In response, the World Foods team is sharing innovative ideas, contacts and ways of bringing the ordinary supermarket customer higher quality goods at cheaper prices. For example, with natural yoghurt, the team has found a new, cheaper high-quality supplier. Now the Chilled Foods team can offer their *non*-ethnic customer good quality, more cost-effective products. The same applies to coconut water and chocolate, through new collaborations with the soft drinks team and confectionary buyers. This is benefiting ailing parts of the business and bringing prices down for the customer.

It is not only buyers who are reaching out to Antonia. Heads of other departments are asking Antonia to help them be more effective leaders. By sharing her own learning, Antonia is now contributing across the core business.

Antonia is thrilled and says she never expected this to happen. But perhaps such success is a well-earned and hard-won reward for Antonia's humility and openness to her own failures and her willingness to experiment with and change her leadership style. There is an important organisational lesson here. It may not be enough to create and spot growth potential. You have to be willing to change yourself, and possibly also the system, in order to achieve it.

Stocking the World Foods aisle: the story of how a global supermarket manager had to relearn how to lead effectively, in a multi-ethnic context

Reflections for leaders

- Tsunamis and hurricanes – how would a literal weather event affect your business or organisation?
- What are you assuming about the meaning or association of your organisation's 'product' for its customers?
- Trusting a fake – what part of your brand signals authenticity and 'home' and for whom?
- When have you learned something about leadership from your employee or even their family?

Reflections for coaches

- Diversity of thinking, diversity of experience, diversity of geography across the team or organisation
- Whole family care – systemic and individual perspectives and subsequent impact
- New core of the organisation – if the core were to shift, what might form the new core, from which others would want to come and learn?
- The leader's narrative – what is it and how do they deploy it?

Names of individuals and organisations have been changed or anonymised.

Note

1 2011 UK Population Census.

References

Berne, E. (1973). *Games People Play: The Basic Handbook of Transactional Analysis*. London: Penguin Books Ltd.

The Guardian. (2007). www.theguardian.com/business/2007/may/16/supermarkets.food

Mintel Survey. (2012). https://store.mintel.com/ethnic-foods-uk-september-2012

Chapter 4

Cooking for conflict resolution

An exploration of difference: how unexpected collaborations can foster greater innovation, creativity and success

We needed something lighter in a programme of invariably serious, often distressing issues. So the textured audio of sizzling onions, herbs being chopped, the clunk and clank of battered saucepans being washed up . . . the pouring of green tea, seemed just the thing.

This chapter takes us into environments of conflict: Traditional thinking, tribal thinking and prejudice in Central Asia. The reader is challenged to explore the notion of collaboration, resistance or avoidance. Businesses constantly call for innovation. They ask their employees to take risks but then do not necessarily tolerate the results if things don't go well. When it comes to diversity many leaders assume an obligation towards it, rather than recognising the competitive advantage of diversity of thought to increase profit (McKinsey & Company 2018), productivity and the long-term survival of their company or team.

To achieve a more constructive, genuine engagement with diversity and its potential to improve business and society, we need to demand fresh thinking from ourselves, stimulate it in others and seek it out from new sources, such as different ethnicity, gender, age, geography or operational specialism. Difference brings breadth and depth of ideas.

Part case study, part experience and part reflections on the commercial efficiency and value-creation of daring to collaborate, this chapter explores the potential at work and in society of embracing difference. It explores resistance to difference of thought, including cultural conditioning and prejudice. It also considers 'stuck' or entrenched thinking, encompassing individual versus collective approaches. The chapter explores how food can be a vehicle for forging greater respect and empathy, observing the business partnership of two Middle Eastern chefs. It also includes my personal attempt to use cooking for conflict resolution.

Cooking for conflict resolution: an exploration of difference: how unexpected collaborations can foster greater innovation, creativity and success

> *We make almost the same spinach soup in my village in the north, as the lady in the Eastern Province of Afghanistan does. I didn't know we are so similar. . .*

Many of my clients ask me to coach them on diversity, collaboration and innovation in a changing, often international context. My first leadership position included national conflict resolution in Afghanistan. It was a daunting prospect, considering that the world's most powerful leaders, whom I considered somewhat more qualified than myself to intervene, as well as the United Nations and combined NATO armed forces had already spent years deployed in the region, attempting this task. I wondered what I could do.

Food is one vehicle to enable harmony and connection, including in a context where people do not have plenty. I believe that food can act as a gateway to developing a shared understanding. It can broaden knowledge between different communities. Food can communicate below the conscious, tackling deeper, more complex issues, such as prejudice, connection or the need for healing.

Kalashnikovs and Kabuli rice

When I worked for the BBC, I was asked to lead a women's media for development aid project in Afghanistan. I created and launched Afghan Woman's Hour, broadcast on BBC World Service Radio, in Dari and Pashto – two of Afghanistan's many national languages. The programme was called Zan wa Jahan Emrouzi, meaning 'Woman in Today's World'. Its remit was to talk about women's rights, health, education and conflict resolution. I sought to empower a local team of Afghan women reporters to bring a range of views [not just a man's view or the government's view, as had been normal for many Afghans until then], to a potential audience of 32.5 million local listeners[1] and approximately 4.7 million people living in the Afghan diaspora.

Afghanistan is divided geographically and ethnically. There are 18 different ethnic tribes – each with their own language, traditional dress and customs. Many of these customs predate Islam by thousands of years. There is a caste-like hierarchy between different communities. Darker skinned Pashtuns of the South are looked down upon by the fairer skinned, chiseled-jaw Tajiks from the north. Both consider themselves superior to the Hazara people, who are recognisable in the street for their more Mongolian facial features. These are just a few examples of ethnic difference but also of cultural prejudice. There are other forms of bias concerning age, gender and the acceptability or inevitability of or permission to carry out violence in the home – including bullying and domestic violence perpetrated against women by women. In addition, the lack of freedom for some women and girls to leave the home, other than for their own wedding or burial.

Afghan Woman's Hour set out to be inclusive, to explore prejudice and create respect. It aimed to create a space to talk openly about real issues that mattered most to women.

I wanted to hear ordinary, uneducated voices telling us what they needed to help them change their lives for the better. I wanted to bring practical help. A source of empowering ideas that could make families living in poverty less hungry – less hungry today, not in three to five years' time following the production of a well-meaning but slow, top-down policy document.

My vision for the programme was for it to become the listener's friend, comfort and confidante. A welcoming, accessible place to express the known but unsayable; a space to feel held and contained in a caring but not an oppressive way. I imagined the potential of a nation of war widows, kidnapped women, sold children, battered wives, burned daughters, to heal each other through sharing their stories, in a trusted space, dedicated to women and girls. I wanted to bring them hope. And a route to emotional and economic self-empowerment. A window on the outside world, for those often cruelly shut off from it. Rather like the coaching relationship, I sought to create a safe environment for people to get out of 'stuck' and approach each other with less fear.

At first, I dismissed the idea of a recipe slot. It fell into the stereotype of radio programmes for women. At the time, 70% of the Afghans were living off less than a dollar a day.[2] Talking about food seemed wholly inappropriate. Then I changed my mind. I had had an idea. What if we could use cooking as a device for conflict resolution?

Additionally, we needed something lighter in a programme of invariably serious, often distressing issues. So the textured audio of sizzling onions, herbs being chopped, the clunk and clank of battered saucepans being washed up . . . the pouring of green tea, seemed just the thing.

Livestock shuffled and squawked in the background, children played in the dirt outside . . . and all the while, my reporters kept on recording . . . and women kept on sharing. Recipe after recipe. I took the conscious decision that all recipes would be cheap, mainly vegetarian, use local ingredients and would be possible to make for families living off less than a dollar a day. The programme also messaged on health benefits and vitamins.

A recipe for Ramadan from the city of Mazar-i-Sharif in the north, a wedding party cake from Kandahar in the south; a girl from Logar Province in the East, telling another schoolchild how to make biscuits. The stirring of green bean soup in a family home in Paktia Province, also in Eastern Afghanistan, heard by the wives and daughters and, it turned out later, also plenty of husbands and sons, hundreds of miles away in Herat, in Western Afghanistan. In addition Afghan refugee communities in Pakistan, Iran, the UK, Germany and the Netherlands also began responding and contributing to the cooking slot on the programme. There seemed to be a particularly large number of 'sabsi' or green vegetables recipes, which I was told were most definitely distinctive from one another. On special feast days like Eid we allowed a meat recipe.

A listener living just over the border in Peshawar, Pakistan, which is home to a huge Afghan refugee community, showed our reporter how she and a female neighbour had a part share of a cow. They made dairy products from its milk and sold them. This could only work together, for apart neither woman could afford the cow. It beautifully demonstrated collaboration, forged by mutual need and a shared endeavour.

They taught their daughters how women can empower themselves through working together. The quality of the family diet, specifically calcium levels in the women of the family, improved, as well as creating a second source of income.

With so little education, and a paucity of nonpartisan information – at the time there were virtually no books or newspapers and a fractured or non-existent distribution system had there been anything recent in print anyway, let alone people able to read it – many communities developed strong prejudices and entrenched beliefs about each other.

I hoped that food could promote a sense of connection instead of division. I imagined the physicality of sourcing, preparing, cooking and eating food had the potential to lift people out of their cognitive headspace, and into a more visceral, limbic core of human feeling. From here, people could start to talk to each other in a new way.

Afghan women seemed to be saying 'yes'. They began ringing the programme to say how much they were learning about each other. How the differences they had assumed were not so. How shared food could potentially indicate shared feelings and values. Women were revealing and then reviewing their thinking to each other. Their diversity was less than they had thought, yet exciting in the variety of ideas it offered them.

For me this was bottom-up social policy making. It celebrated difference with dignity and enjoyment, which brings so much potential for healing on a personal, national or environmental level; it also offers potential for greater trade and industrial success.

Cooking was the start of 'a conversation' or a connection – one on the air. Despite being so obviously public, the broadcasting space was also an intimate space. One that dipped right into people's homes, hearts and minds. It provided a connection between Afghans at home trying to navigate a fractured society. It also offered a vehicle for Afghans scattered across a diaspora, seeking a link with home, each other and with those in their new communities abroad. And probably plenty more, within homes across Afghanistan and the Afghan radio audiences in the diaspora communities of Iran, the UK, the Netherlands, Germany and the USA. The examples of cooking for conflict resolution show the potential of a conversation to shift belief, conversations which might enable people to speak to each other. Through contributing to the cooking slot, or the discussion it created within communities, listeners started seeing the potential to generate more together, rather than apart.

The business of difference

Diversity. A word supposedly well understood in the business world. Widely used, but often to mean so little. Instead of connoting minority interests – which the majority assume do not apply to them – diversity could instead express the deep potential for richness, learning, discussion and discovery. Indeed sometimes it can sometimes feel as if the notion of diversity is something that is generously offered by the majority to the few, rather than normative and integrated.

Diversity of *thought*. Learning from the diverse experiences of others. Developing a truly global mindset. The opportunity for nurturing world-class thinking. Ideas from every perspective you can think of: The thinking of women, of a rugby player, of a Latin American; of a tribal chief in Africa or from the lowest castes in India. The thinking of homosexuals, heterosexuals, the formally educated or the self-educated.

Imagine a boardroom containing so much knowledge and different experiences. Imagine the ideas you don't have now, but that you could have. The cultural knowledge and the different, conscious perspectives your company would suddenly have access to. Imagine the learning, and with that, the kind of staff you could attract and the offerings they could develop for the customer. Consider the potential for new growth, greater resilience and sustainable successes, through *new thinking*. Diversity could save money and generate new income streams.

How energising all this sounds. But despite recent research findings to the contrary (McKinsey & Company 2018), not every leader believes that their organisation would be more productive or profitable if were more diverse. Some might argue that not every Chinese company needs input from a European for example. Or that a British or American company cannot succeed without the help of Asian or African staff. The same was once said – and in some cases continues to be said – about the need for women in the workplace.

I believe that greater inclusivity increases the cognitive diversity and breadth of thinking in organisations. In other words, different kinds of people deliver different kinds of ideas, approaches and thought processes. Cognitive diversity may bring complexities and may sometimes take more time to navigate. But it is a valuable resource. One which might also cut through lengthy policy making or tangled decision making, through its freshness and clarity of thinking. In other words, diverse viewpoints may speed things up.

Convincing others of the imperative to diversify – be that product related or in terms of recruiting a variety of types of worker – can be draining and dispiriting for leaders who lack a supportive company culture. Senior leaders need their peers and reports to join their vision. For junior staff who feel excluded or see others excluded, championing greater inclusion in a corporate environment that doesn't intend to change can be disillusioning. They may fear that championing their views may limit their careers instead of enhancing productivity.

Achieving diversity can be challenging. In some environments it can feel like pushing a barrel of water uphill whilst wearing high-heeled shoes. I certainly remember some of my ideas for diversity at work, receiving a reaction of utter silence. I now know to think of this as a broader systemic insight rather than just one individual leader's thinking, although it might be that too. It can be difficult to know where to take one's enthusiasm, particularly when one is working at a junior level. For senior leaders who feel they are running into a brick wall, the challenge must be equally frustrating and contrary to their values.

Leaders and employees must watch for their own reactions when things do not progress as they would like. It could become easy to complain and criticise others for being unenlightened or unfashionable in their thinking. But this very thinking risks reverse intolerance, a failure of those wanting change to afford some degree of tolerance and understanding towards those who do not – those with a different view.

People can become fed up with repeated mantras about change if they are content with or better served by the status quo. Welcoming difference can be threatening. It involves risk. It requires openness. Resistance may mask prejudice and inherited social conditioning. Or it may expose it. Such acknowledged or unacknowledged bias can be active, passive or even subconscious.

When people feel beleaguered in their difference, a consequence can be apathy or even depression. Their belief and trust that change is possible slumps. An organisational slide into the stasis of collective thinking and resigned assumption, entrenched beliefs, disconnection, 'stuckness'.

In some competitive corporate or sports environments, collaboration between diverse individuals or groups of individuals is best avoided or even against the rules. But where it is allowed, people sometimes fear or fail to connect across boundaries; they fear or fail to think imaginatively enough. Thus, opportunities for success and joy at work may be lost. There is also a risk that awareness in society will be lost.

The individual versus the collective view

Groups of people or teams think together – 'nous' or 'we' thinking – in a way that is different from the thinking we achieve on our own (Ringer 2017). Today's individualistic Western society may have forgotten that humans belonged to collectives long before couples and nuclear families became a social norm. In contrast, many of today's African, Asian and Latin American communities continue to think collectively, as 'we' before or instead of 'I'.

However, the collective can stifle diversity of opinion. It can evidence entrenched attitudes just as much as when individuals share a non-shifting or 'stuck' points of view. Groups can affirm each other's thinking and diminish dissenting or different viewpoints. However, the notion of 'nous' thinking suggests that the way we think and the outcome of thinking together is different – and possibly more adventurous than when we cogitate alone.

There is so much scope for conflict on a micro or on a macro scale, because of notions of identity linked to perceptions of difference. Different countries, counties, cantons and regions, different tribes, castes, social classes and family groupings. Around the world there is a wealth of different languages, musical tradition and dress; customs around food, religion and social norms; communities known to have expertise in hunting or gathering, others which excel in retail or mechanics, storytelling, law making or academia.

And so to the corporate context, where it is essential to ask ourselves how the way we were brought up in a family, cultural or community context informs how we think, feel and act at work – rather like stirring a soup of harmony and conflict, containing simultaneously difference, prejudice and beliefs we may be quite attached to – it is there we find what we have in common. Different points of view or experiences may predictably or unexpectedly divide or unite us. We must also carry a conscious awareness that we may never discover every point of similarity nor reconcile every degree of difference between individuals or groups of individuals.

Swapping recipes and creating new ones

There are examples of bridge-building projects around the globe which aim to resolve conflict and bring people closer together. People who want sometimes remarkably similar things: To live in peace, find a job and bring up their families. Food represents an inspiring metaphor for this sentiment at Ottolenghi, a London restaurant chain founded by two chefs: One is Israeli, the other Palestinian. They are business partners not personal partners, who were brought up in different suburbs of Jerusalem, across political and social divides.

The pair say they would never have met – or perhaps been *able* to meet – had they not come to London to go to chef school (Ottolenghi and Tamimi 2012). Once in the UK, they discovered a shared passion for the foods that they were brought up with, and the potential to create new dishes through thinking and working together. Exemplifying explicitly the ideas of 'nous' or 'us' thinking. As colleagues they have established a string of successful restaurants, which they oversee personally, daily. They consciously retain a close connection to their staff, their business and the responses of their customers to the food that is created in their kitchens.

Ottolenghi and Tamimi believe that their geography of birth informs who they are:

> *Yes, we still think of Jerusalem as our home. Not home in the sense of the place you conduct your daily life, or constantly return to. In fact, Jerusalem is our home almost against our wills. It is our home because it defines us, whether we like it or not . . . we explore our own culinary DNA . . . inspired by the richness of a city with 4,000 years of history, that has changed hands endlessly and that now stands as the centre of three massive faiths and is occupied by residents of such utter diversity.*
>
> (Ottolenghi and Tamimi 2012)

Meeting outside their geographical, political, family and cultural contexts may have allowed chefs Ottolenghi and Tamimi to leverage both their commonality and their differences. Enabling them to meet, think, decide, plan and take action.

Ottolenghi and Tamimi may not have intended their culinary partnership to act as an inspirational role model for bridge building and conflict resolution. But

I see it as role modelling just that. This partnership across difference shows the potential of people to explore difference, disconnect and, sometimes including inherited enmity, to find instead an energising 'togetherness'.

Closing thoughts

Leaders may think they are 'diversity aware'. Others may have no interest in it, but feel they ought to evidence something in this arena, lest it impact negatively on their careers. Leaders need to remain creative thinkers. They must question themselves about where their thinking has become repetitive, lacking in diversity or formulaic.

Leaders need to look after their energy and optimism levels, to stay resilient and generate fresh thinking. In demanding innovative thinking from others, leaders must be aware of the need to offer a genuine receptacle for that thinking. They may be avoidant of suggestions which throw everything up in the air; excuses to oneself about some ideas being too disruptive, draining or demanding excess attention may be just that – excuses – rather than *reasons* to shut them out or shut them down.

There is also the risk that when an employee comes up with a great idea that is a bit 'different', this helpful act may compromise an already exhausted executive, who would rather zip home for some dinner. Leaders must also acknowledge the cost of taking risks or evolving a new collaboration: that of risk and reward.

Competition rules make some forms of inter-corporate collaboration impossible, even illegal. Confidentiality and conflict of interest are relevant here too. But there is plenty of opportunity and potential for collaboration that is not being exploited. However, to ask if it were exploited or at least explored, what matrix of creativity could result, informing both the bottom line (McKinsey & Company 2018), levels of productivity and happiness at work?

The happiness generated by Afghan women sharing recipes across the geographical and tribal divides of their impoverished nation was an unexpected joy. The combination of potential health improvement amidst economic strife, together with an honest and spontaneous reappraisal of prejudice, entrenched conflict and areas of commonality, generated much cheer. It reduced perceptions of distance through difference. Instead people said they felt emotionally closer, now willing and able to approach each other with a warmth of regard – a better formula for a traumatised and suffering population than maintaining high levels of stress through enmity.

Cooking is only one way of approaching conflict resolution. There are many others. Leaders must meet conflict where it is, rather than try to contain and quieten it. They need to think about inclusion and where they assume they are inclusive but are not.

Identifying currently untapped resources within an organisation or industry sector, for potential collaboration, could be tried. Previously unacknowledged or excluded cultures, communities, sub-cultures and specialist groups in and around the office, factory or refugee camp, could be invited in to stimulate new thinking and bring cognitive diversity. Every leader can ask what they can do differently.

They can ask the same of individuals in their team. Approaches to diversity can also be applied at home not just at work.

Trying to influence diversity from the bottom up can be draining and cause despondency, if senior leaders are not interested in engaging with their conscious or unconscious bias. Also dispiriting is when senior leaders who are convinced that diversity in the workplace brings greater efficiency and effectiveness meet resistance above and below them.

Changing mindsets is about openness and flexibility. All sides need support to remain resilient in the face of explicit obstruction and setbacks. It is important to note that when asking for tolerance towards others, we may in turn be displaying intolerance towards those who are yet to be convinced of a different point of view.

It is inspiring to think what could be achieved at home or in a global corporate context if leaders sought out vehicles for unity and connection; if they created conversations between diverse groups of people that produced amazing ideas, products or solutions. If we regarded ourselves as part of a social and professional mosaic of varied thinking, what would it now be possible to co-create?

Cooking for conflict resolution: an exploration of difference: how unexpected collaborations can foster greater innovation, creativity and success

Reflections for leaders

- what is your definition of **diversity?**
- what is your definition of **difference?**
- what is your definition of **inclusivity?**
- what is your definition of **conflict?**
- what is your definition of **collaboration?**
- what is your definition of **conversation?**
- what is your definition of **diaspora** in the context of your home and/or working life?

Reflections for coaches

- What sources of nourishment or ideas are there at work?
- What sources of nourishment through diversity are yet to be tapped for ideas or solutions?
- When have you dared to include?
- When do you resist collaboration?
- What conscious bias are you prepared to acknowledge?
- What subconscious bias may you be carrying? What bias would you be ashamed to admit?
- What dish or food from your culture would you share – and what would it communicate about you or your thinking?

Notes

1 Source UNDP 2016: www.af.undp.org/content/afghanistan/en/home/countryinfo/
2 According to the UN, 35% of Afghans live below the poverty line www.af.undp.org/content/afghanistan/en/home/countryinfo/

References

Afghanistan Fact Sheet UNDP. (2016). www.af.undp.org/content/afghanistan/en/home/countryinfo/

McKinsey & Company. (2018). *Delivering Through Diversity*. www.mckinsey.com/business-functions/organization/our-insights/delivering-through-diversity

Ottolenghi, Y. and Tamimi, S. (2012). *Jerusalem*. London: Ebury Press (p. 9).

Ringer, M. (2017). *Thinking in Groups and Teams: Surfacing New Thoughts*. Edited by Martin Ringer Authors: Rob Gordon, Martin Ringer, Robert D. Hinshelwood, Rosaleen Tamaki, Richard Morgan-Jones, Barry Jones, Robert French, Peter Simpson Mario Perini, Francesco Comelli, Silvia Corbella, Simone Schirinzi (pp. 5–11). www.argo-onlus.it/wp-content/uploads/2015/01/ringeredizspeciale.pdf

Suggested reading

Ryde, J. (2009). *Being White in the Helping Professions: Developing Effective Intercultural Awareness*. London: Jessica Kingsley Publishers.

Chapter 5

Coaching across multiple cultures

Confronting stereotypes in the coach-leader relationship

I got the worst coach, the youngest coach and a woman.

This chapter recounts the experiences and attitudes of a 40-something Sudanese coaching client, who felt she'd been assigned 'the worst coach' in her organisation's international leadership development programme. It explores the client's underlying cultural conditioning against speaking about feelings, including work-related challenges. In addition, it investigates her psychological 'attack' on the quality and credibility of the coach she was allocated, me.

I considered the client's directness about this surprisingly 'Western'. She is highly educated, fluent in multiple languages and passionate about her work to improve the lives of women and children. In the end, the coaching relationship was a success; I would argue that this was only possible because I was able to contain the attack rather than feel upset by it. Thus, I was able to retain a curiosity about what might underpin the client's assumptions and reactions, rather than revert to defensiveness on my part.

This is a story of coaching across multiple cultures simultaneously. One might use the analogy of a constellation: the dance of different planets, orbiting at different speeds in different directions and with sometimes different intention, yet sharing the same universe.

Coaching across multiple cultures simultaneously

In a country that's not your country, you can even walk naked.
[Sudanese saying]

A Kenyan accountant posted to Kabul. A Bangladeshi poverty specialist, married to a Mexican, working in New York. A South African IT expert of Chinese descent living in Uganda. A Canadian in Chad. And a Venezuelan-born Croatian stationed in an office in Switzerland. This was a truly multi-national and multi-cultural assignment.

I was asked to join a coaching team, accompanying a group of global executives working in the Third Sector, in an international leadership development programme. Our job was to help them apply their learning. To my mind, in contrast to our clients, we looked disappointingly homogenous: mostly white, mostly female, mostly middle class, mostly English.

My Sudanese client said:

> *When I saw the line-up of coaches on the first day, I thought, I want that older man, with the white hair. In my culture, he would be the best coach. And then I got you. The youngest one – and a woman!*

We began with enquiring about her culture and community, including conscious and unconscious bias. Included is what can be said to an outsider and what can only be expressed within one's own culture.

> *'The worst coach,'* I said, leaning forwards, smiling.
> *'Yes, exactly!'*, responded Amina, now also laughing whilst retaining what looked to me like sincere aggression:
> *'I was assigned the worst coach!'*

Amina is in her 40s. She is a Sudanese Muslim, currently working in Syria. Amina comes from an enormous extended family of hundreds of relatives. There is nothing unusual about that in her culture. What is unusual is that Amina is not married. She does not have children. These are two culturally unacceptable choices, which she points out to me.

Our meeting was her first encounter with Executive Leadership Coaching. It was to be a journey of honesty and challenging cultural exchanges, embracing difference, judgement, prejudice and sexism. Amina explains:

> *I must admit, I was very stressed about our first meeting. I thought, how am I going to talk openly to a stranger for an hour and a half!? You see, in my culture, going to a psychiatrist is acceptable. But not a coach or counsellor. If you want counselling or mentoring, you go to your siblings, your auntie or your neighbour. It's a very challenging concept, to open up to a person from outside one's community.*

Amina decided the coaching would only work for her if she didn't filter her thinking before sharing it with me. This exemplified why having a coach from a different culture served her better:

> *It made it easier for me. It gave us freedom. In Sudan, we have a saying: 'In a country that's not your country, you can even walk naked.' Within my own community, one is afraid to be open, because of being judged. As my coach, you didn't judge me. You created a safe space for me. I could talk to you about issues because you are not from my culture.*

It was not long before, during a Skype session, Amina joyously declared:

> *I have the best coach for me! You are actually very good at your job!*

I asked Amina what I did right, from a cultural perspective, that enabled our coaching relationship to be successful. She repeated the importance of not being judged. Of being listened to with sincerity and sympathy. Of reflecting back what she said but resisting giving or imposing advice. She felt respected:

> *You listened with your heart. I felt your sincerity and sympathy. You made the coaching feel human. Sometimes we laughed. You revealed a bit about yourself. That exchange of information, meant I felt less embarrassed. I felt more connection. I felt you felt what I'm feeling.*

It was unusual for me to share a little about myself. Normally I do not. But in this case, I made a cultural judgement and took the risk. In terms of deepening rapport, it seems to have worked.

One could argue that reflecting back, not judging and good listening are standard, best practice coaching skills that any coach, working face to face or virtually, anywhere in the world should offer. But Amina also cited commonality as another reason for success of the coaching relationship:

> *You had worked in Peshawar in Pakistan, where I used to work. I believe your exposure to different cultures in a meaningful way – not just being a tourist on holiday – helped you understand me better.*

Invariably the coach must hold the dynamic tension between being similar enough on a human and/or professional level to gain credibility as a coach, whilst avoiding the risk of collusion.

For Amina, warmth of rapport and relationship was an important investment, over and above the mechanics of getting on with the coaching. That is not to say that I allowed unfocused chatting to seep into the coaching session. Rather, I sought to understand her culture and to allow plenty of time for her to teach me about her upbringing and how it informs how she thinks. For Amina, coaching was a new concept for her to acclimatise to.

She felt ill at ease with my boundaries around time. She found the nature of this professional relationship, however warm and respectful, rather calculated:

> *Your coach is not like a friend you can call in the middle of the night. I found that difficult. When it was the end of a coaching session, it felt transactional. I had to culturally understand this and adjust to your culture.*

Amina's story is just one account from a thousands-strong community of international aid workers, who work within and across multiple, simultaneous different cultural systems. A Third Sector leader may be born in one country, raised and educated in another and posted every couple of years to field stations in several more. Some are married to people from different backgrounds, raising children across an international school system. Many are required to work and be coached in one or more foreign languages.

Even within one organisation, there can be multiple cultures in operation. Think of the contrast between a hot, dusty, rural field station and a steel and glass headquarters in a busy metropolis, thousands of miles away. Consider also, the potential cultural similarities and differences of the core clients, caught up in a humanitarian crisis be it in the cities and villages of Africa, Asia, Russia or Latin America.

It is this multi-cultural mash up that prompted me to reflect on how many cultures are in play, when coaching international leaders. It is a complex and fascinating matrix of differences, all at play, all at once.

Earlier I mentioned the apparently culturally dull line up of coaches. But look beneath the surface and the group includes one coach who was born in Iraq and raised in Iran and the UK, one who discovered coaching in rural India and another who was posted to Afghanistan. One coach adopted a son from China. Another is an expert on German and Israeli banks. The cultural offering has the potential to go wider and deeper, if one then considers who supervises each coach. And what else informs that coach's professional and personal journey? This includes narratives of mixed marriages, moving to a new country and complete career change; of creativity, resilience and personal crisis.

Whether it is the coach's story or the coaching client's story, this interconnected 'dance' of influences reminded me of Peter Hawkins' '7-eyed Model of Supervision'. He recently re-created it into a 10-eyed model of coaching, mentoring and organisational consulting (Hawkins and Smith 2013). Professor Hawkins believes coaches need to explore the cultural conflict within the client i.e., where they were born, brought up, educated etc. and how each influences them as a person and as a leader. In addition, both coach and client need to explicitly examine their cultural assumptions about each other:

> *A Western coach might ask about ambition. They're likely to mean achievement from an individualistic perspective. That's a Western concept. If the*

> *client is Asian, they may well answer it from a collective perspective, framed as 'what my family or community needs me to achieve'.*
>
> [Peter Hawkins]

Peter Hawkins, who describes himself as white and British, recalls a piece of work he delivered for a mental health organisation in the West Indies. It started off with a distinct atmosphere of unease:

> *When I walked into the room, the man I was to be working alongside said: 'Ah Peter Hawkins . . . Hawkins . . . that's an interesting name . . .' Hawkins was the name of one of the first slave traders and slave owners on the island . . . I didn't know that. The client [who was of colour] also had a slave owner's name. Like mine, it was not an African one.*

For Hawkins, these were powerful and disturbing connotations. Connotations of dominance and oppression. This represented the opposite of the neutral base most coaches seek to start off with. How challenging to attempt to empower the client, from this historically loaded first encounter.

The result of this meeting caused Hawkins to demand that coaches consider what baggage they carry into the room before they even start coaching. To notice what they may not have been aware of culturally. Coaches need to consider the cultural content of their client, themselves, their coach supervisor. It is particularly important that the coach is from the dominant culture. Many white Caucasian people do not think of themselves as a colour. Many are not even aware of this. What vital aspects of what the client expresses might be missed or misunderstood because there is too much or too little cultural similarity?

Working with Third Sector leaders is a chance to consider the concept of a 'global citizen'. These are international leaders who are on the move. They make and break multiple attachments as they follow postings from country to country. Coaching Third Sector leaders is not like a Brit coaching a German or an American working with someone Asian. Coaching global citizens requires the coach to consider multiple cultures simultaneously: The home culture, a person's faith, their partner's background, the corporate culture and their regional posting. All these ingredients and sources of experience and learning need attention, because of their potential to influence the client's growth, behaviour choices and impact.

A colleague and coach on the same leadership programme, Carole Pemberton, told me that one of her clients had never had a drink with his boss. He could not. That is because he is Muslim and he will not go somewhere that serves alcohol. His boss did not realise this. Imagine the potential to limit career advancement in a competitive organisation and the dip in self-confidence when an employee is inadvertently excluded.

Another coaching client told Pemberton that she reminded him of his mother. It was a message about huge respect for the coach. The client enjoyed the quality of her listening. It was not an oedipal thing for the client, but it was for Pemberton, who carried her Western cultural assumptions into the coaching space:

> *Internally, I panicked. When he said I reminded him of his mother, I was so bewildered, wondering what had I done to create a mother-child-client dynamic? The quality of my coaching went out of the window. All my energy became focused on myself. I was anxious. Completely distracted.*

Only when Pemberton had calmed her inner dialogue was she able to attend to her client again. He was saying he felt safe and supported to think for himself.

Carole Pemberton reflects on the benefits to her coaching of having adopted a Chinese-born son:

> *The distance between me and my clients from different cultures has reduced because I now live with difference.*

Coaching across multiple cultures simultaneously, it is worth considering the coach matching process, including the ability of the coach to establish trust and rapport virtually with a client they may never be able to meet face to face.

When coaching internationally, particularly in volatile regions, sessions can be cancelled at a moment's notice because a bomb has gone off, there has been a siege, a government crackdown, or a violent storm has brought the phone lines down. These are just a few of the practical considerations which can annoy a coach who has protected time in their diary, only to find their client does not make it to the session.

On an emotional level, coaches need to be psychologically robust yet remain connected to self. They must be able to tolerate hearing their clients recount difficult, sometimes traumatising experiences. It is a balance of compassion and resilience.

Closing thoughts

Coaches working transculturally need to coach shoulder to shoulder with their client. With multi-cultural coaching, it is worth considering all coaching as 'group coaching', even if there are only two people in the room. It is no good coaching despite the client's system – be that their office structures or the multiple cultures at play for them at work. Coaches need to bring the whole 'constellation' of cultural ingredients into the room.

Instead of trying to diminish differences coaches should instead seek them out, seek to highlight where there is difference, even if it is not obviously apparent. We should seek to inquire about how differences – both external and internal – inform the client's thinking, behaviour choices and leadership.

Working with Amina from Sudan illustrates the importance of acknowledging cultural stereotypes from outsiders looking in, but also from people within their own culture looking out. Coaching is a chance to encourage leaders to see every individual as unique, rather than as part of a national, religious or organisational collective. When coaching across multiple different cultures at the same time, coaches might challenge themselves to hold two stances in mind – the value of uniqueness but also that of human universality and interconnectedness.

Reflections for leaders

- 'Walking naked' – what can you say outside your organisation or team that you cannot say within it?
- What would you say to a friend in the middle of the night about your work issue?
- What kind of community is your top team?
- Where are there cultural barriers?
- What kind of community do you want to create for your employees?
- What cultural baggage or assumptions do you bring into the room?
- What cultural baggage did you not realise you bring into the room?
- Individuality versus human universality

Reflections for coaches

- Seek to explore, not diminish, difference
- Whose culture is 'dominant'?
- What cultural baggage do you carry – what might you not be conscious of?
- Consider the concept that all individual coaching, when working across multiple cultures, is in fact group coaching
- Check for cultural stereotypes on both sides, i.e., both client and coach
- Walking naked – what can your client say in their coaching session but not outside?
- When do you as a coach 'walk naked', i.e. express yourself in a way you don't in other parts of your life?
- Ask about meaning of an experience – do not assume you understand what the client means from what they are saying

Reference

Hawkins, P. and Smith, N. (2013). Chapter 15: Trans-Cultural Coaching. In *Coaching, Mentoring and Organisational Consultancy*. London: Open University Press.

Suggested reading

Pemberton, C. (2015). *Resilience: A Practical Guide for Coaches*. London: McGraw Hill Education, Open University Press.

Ride, J. (2009). *Being White in the Helping Professions: Developing Effective Intercultural Awareness*. London: JKP.

Chapter 6

Leading behind bars

Insights from inside. Leadership learning from a former prison governor who says in terms of crime, he could have 'gone either way'

> *There were flames shooting everywhere, staff were dragging prisoners out, they were giving them mouth to mouth resuscitation . . . the prison officers were incredibly brave. A prison riot is about life and death. It's not like a tricky meeting. I think what a lot of people describe as difficult management is about First World problems . . . like 'I'm in Waitrose supermarket and they've run out of anchovies.'*

In this chapter we see how Phil, a leader working in a male prison environment in the UK, accesses insights from his troubled childhood, as a resource to do his job better. Phil embraces multiple aspects of his leadership role, from dealing with violence within a prison to convincing employers to give convicted criminals the chance of a job.

Phil hired me as his coach three times. He found the coaching space gave him a much needed, confidential sounding board. It helped him externalise his thinking. The coaching opportunity also steadied him as a leader when some of the feelings evoked by his troubled upbringing threatened to interfere with his focus and resilience at work. Phil found having a space to process personal, systemic or political stressors enabled him to direct his mental energy into generating solutions, to better understand cycles of crime and to learn more about those who break the law.

This chapter offers leaders who may never have experienced a criminal justice system context, a glimpse of prison life. Insights include themes of respect, power and despair, of rehabilitation, the desire to rescue and judgement of others. From a leadership perspective this chapter examines the challenge of developing others and concerns itself with how to be a reflective leader rather than a directive one, especially during emergencies. It charts a journey through childhood, personal and professional choices.

Coaches can consider the notion of parallel process and explore when assumptions or a leader's self-limiting beliefs mirror what might be going on organisationally. The concept of prison as a hidden world or an exclusive space might also be explored.

Leading behind bars: insights from inside. Leadership learning from a former prison governor who says in terms of crime, he could have 'gone either way'

Resilience is the ability to endure. It's not about bouncing back. It's about being able to endure anything that comes at you and just keep going.

Childhood roots

As a senior leader in the British prison system, Phil offers his personal definition of resilience. He grew up on a council estate and would return home from school to find his mother and a group of drunken strangers, rolling around the living room floor waiting for the pub to re-open. There were no books. Nobody cooked any meals. There was no stability. When friends came round to ask Phil out to play, he felt a huge sense of shame.

When, aged 16, Phil's friends started leaving school and going into the building trade, he felt fearful and confused about his own career plans. School was his only safe place. His English teacher suggested that if he didn't know what job he wanted to do, he could stay on to do an 'A' level:

> *Miss Jones was great. She made me believe in myself. I said only posh kids did 'A' levels. Miss Jones said: 'Of course you can do an "A" level . . . and then you need to go and get two more [to qualify to go university]'. So, I stayed on at school. I did Economics, English and Biology. It was transformational doing 'A' levels. Nobody in my family had ever done 'A' levels. I went from feeling like the outside loner, lacking confidence and thinking I'd never amount to anything in the world, to being at university.*

After graduating, Phil joined a graduate fast-track programme to work in prisons. Phil says he could have gone either way. Half his school mates went to work, the other half went into crime – usually petty crime, stealing car radios.

One day Phil was walking down a prison corridor when he saw a couple of his old school friends. They were 'inside'. He had done sport with one of them at school. He was a kind, quiet guy. He had a girlfriend. She was into drugs. He started. She could control her habit but he could not control his. Phil's friend became addicted to heroin and began drug dealing to fund his habit. Phil subtly ushered the two men into his office and made them a cup of tea:

> *We sat chatting as people on very different sides of a fence,' he says.' I had to be careful though. It would have been dangerous to show any favouritism. It would be very bad for my friends if the other prisoners knew I'd been at school with them.*

In prison, there are rules that operate beyond and behind the law. Prisoners must learn how to navigate internal power structures to survive and avoid attack. After the cup of tea, Phil put his friends back behind bars in their cells. He had to lock them up.

Bumping into these two classmates reinforced for Phil the concept of possibility. He believes that any one of us could end up in prison. He maintains that these two men were not awful, violent, difficult people. They had stumbled into a world with negative consequences. They were incredulous that they had ended up in prison.

A good proportion of murderers have never committed a crime before. Phil tells me that killing someone may be their first offence. Usually an argument gets out of hand, anger rises and then suddenly violence erupts, of a nature probably nobody intended. This demonstrates the capacity of any human being to 'go wrong' and malfunction:

> *It's the potential to drift into criminal behaviour, or lose one's temper massively and end up killing someone. When people refer to prisoners as 'scum of the earth,' I'm appalled. Prisoners are people.*

At the core of Phil's personal and leadership ethos is respect, empathy and understanding. It is the ability to see the human above everything else:

> *Understanding where prisoners are coming from is critical. The one thing you must never do as a leader is judge the people behind the cell door. That's because it could have been you. In the right circumstances, any of us are capable of doing things we'd never have dreamed of. . . .*

Showing respect is another of Phil's core values. He recalls chatting to a member of staff in the Prison Wing Office:

> *A prisoner walked by and this prison officer said 'fuck off'. The prisoner continued walking. There was such contempt. Speaking like that to a prisoner conveys that they're such an utterly worthless human being, that the officer couldn't bring himself to speak to him decently.*

Phil instructs his prison officers not to hide behind their uniforms:

> *What you're likely to get back is a prisoner who'll potentially punch you in the face and tell you to fuck off.*

This illustration of power differences and conduct is so evident in a prison setting. Phil insists that his staff realise how what they say can hugely impact a person. He urges that we should not assume that a small gesture has only a small consequence. Nor think that a significant act will have an equally significant effect. Here is an example of that small gesture concept. The prison team was doing a cell search. There was a suicide watch on one particular prisoner. A staff member found a diary entry which read:

Today was the day I was going to kill myself. Then a prison officer opened the door and said 'good morning, how are you doing?' Just that reaching out to me, to ask me how I am, made me feel he's bothered about me. . . . He asked how I am. . . .

This seemingly superficial interaction may have been the difference between life and death for a prisoner who was feeling bleak about their situation. Prison staff have obvious power. They are free go home at night. They also have inadvertent power over prisoners' lives, including unconscious power. For example, a prison officer may not think they particularly matter to the prisoners they are in charge of. But to a person behind bars, a staff member can represent their whole existence, as Phil explains:

You lock and unlock their door. You have the power to decide when they can have a shower or a loo roll. You're the one who puts in a job application for them.

So, we can see how prison staff can exercise their powers to oppress and humiliate – including exercising their need to act out their own experiences of authoritarian behaviour, which may have occurred earlier in their lives. We also see how the power of a prison officer can be used to promote dignity, self-respect and hope.

The business of drugs, debt and despair

In prisons, there is intrinsic corruption, bullying and power through gang membership. Inside, there are inmates who control the supply of tobacco or drugs. Some make big money. Their businesses spurn rival gangs within the prison, escalating levels of risk and violence. Prisons can become dangerous places:

That's why I never turn a blind eye to drugs in prisons. Absolutely not. Prisoners who are stoned on cannabis aren't violent, but the people supplying the drugs are. Synthetic, novel psychoactive substances, like Spice, which is created in a lab, have a much worse effect. The result is a rise in violence, with more extreme, even more unpredictable behaviour from prisoners.

Despite the bravado, many prisoners are often acutely afraid. They fear being physically attacked because they have got into debt and cannot pay back what they owe. Prisoners borrow tobacco, biscuits, coffee, drugs. In prison, the interest rate is 100% a day. Naive new arrivals may be offered a cigarette. They feel so emotionally low that they accept, not realising that they are now obliged to pay back two cigarettes. Those who cannot pay find they owe four cigarettes a day later, then eight the following day. Life inside prison can be a brutal game continued by violent gangs, politics, desperation and debt.

Prisoners are looking for escapism from their feelings of misery in that minute, as Phil explains:

> *We tell prisoners when they arrive, not to get into debt. But prisoners have usually never thought through the consequences of their actions. That's why they've ended up in prison. So, if they're feeling a bit down, they're worried about the hit right now from that cigarette. They're not thinking how to pay it back. When it's not a cigarette but drugs they're after, you can multiply that drive by 100.*

Just as there are cycles of criminal behaviour in society, which see a person commit a crime, be convicted, imprisoned, then released and soon reoffend, so there are repeated patterns of behaviour within prison life. For example, cycles of debt. If a prisoner incurs unmanageable levels of debt in one wing, they ask for a transfer to another prison or to go to the segregation unit, such is their fear of attack.

Many prisoners who are moved to a different prison, do it all over again. This brings to mind Freud's notion of the 'death drive' (Freud 1920) – compulsive, destructive repetition of behaviours, even if they have negative consequences. Also, Kolb's learning cycle (Kolb 2015), which offers a model of learning something new, experimenting with the new input, evaluating it and then integrating or rejecting it, ready for the next new piece of information. It appears that some prisoners fail to cognitively integrate their experiences. They go round the learning cycle again and again, *not learning.*

Prisoners who fail to master survival on the 'inside' end up endangering their friends and family, as their debt problem seeps into the broader community outside prison. To rescue the debt relatives are asked to put money into the bank account of one of the prison gang leaders. If that relative can't pay, then the prisoner who's incurred the debt will be beaten up. If things escalate, a relative may receive a 'visit from somebody'. In other words, they are threatened with intimidation or physical violence.

The leadership skill and dexterity required to steer both prisoners and prison staff through such a threatening environment seems immense. Senior leaders need to retain their resilience but also help junior prison staff develop theirs. Remaining resilient demands both emotional connection and empathy with what is going on, as well as the ability to self-monitor and to be tough or rather, firmly boundaried, without becoming aggressive nor emotionally shutting down. I shall return to the theme of resilience in the next part of this chapter, which addresses crisis.

Leading through crisis

Phil knows how to manage crises, such as a prison riot, from first-hand experience. He has also learned how to lead remotely in crisis, being in charge of those handling an out of control situation directly on site. Both stances present stressful leadership challenges:

Prison crises can be acutely risky, dangerous and violent situations with prisoners smashing the prison up and refusing to be locked in their cells. Things can escalate and end up with a murder.

Phil describes one particular incident:

When I arrived at the scene, there were two hundred men hanging around, out of their cells. There was blood everywhere. The staff were afraid. They wanted leadership and reassurance that they'd be safe. The wing needed to be secured for the police forensics team to go in. After we'd dealt with everything, got the prisoners back under our control and mopped up all the blood, we had a staff meeting. It was 2am.

That night, as in other emergency situations, Phil split practical and emotional tasks. He also split off from himself, in order to function in the moment. During the crisis, Phil saw himself dealing with staff and prisoners, as if from the outside. Only later did he process the horrors of what he had seen and the fears he had for his own and others' safety:

You switch into this professional mode – you become 'the governor'. You're not like a normal human being, seeing a dead body in the street . . . at that point you don't see the body as a 'person'.

Phil knows he cannot escape dealing with his own fears and unprocessed emotions. One of the consequences is that he is now able to better manage the stress of emergencies. He becomes snappy, tense and short-fused with people in the days straight after an incident that he has led. Through increased self-awareness, his ability to accurately assess his feelings and behaviours allows him to monitor his stress levels more effectively. He knows when he needs a few days off work. At these times, he walks the dog a lot and focuses on taking his children to school. He is responding to mental and bodily signs indicating to him that he needs to prioritise his personal wellbeing.

In another incident, Phil was in charge at arm's length, guiding a live situation with national implications. The unrest started, as it almost always does, in the evening. Prison staff inevitably end up working into the early hours of the morning. Because riots carry a mob mentality, with prisoners loaded up on drugs 'losing it' and breaking into the prison pharmacy in the hope of obtaining more, Phil will receive a report that fires have been started inside the prison. As the remote lead, he must give the final order for the riot squad to go in. Front of mind, is that someone might die.

We brought in 60 extra emergency staff and needed 100 extra cells for prisoners who'd smashed theirs up. We had to find spare cells in different parts of the country. When you're leading remotely, you're almost blind. You're told what's going on and you may be making life and death decisions. You have authority to say whether staff can intervene. Any of those men [male prisoners] might try and kill your staff. You're trying to approve the plans in front of you, assessing and reassessing a moving situation hour by hour, based on your own experience.

As a leader, you're sitting there at command HQ holding your breath. You know you can't keep telephoning your leaders, but you know your local commander may not have managed this kind of situation before. They need reassurance that they're doing right thing. And you know sometimes they're not.

At times it may seem easier or obvious to resort to command and control style leadership behaviours. But that must be offset against allowing your staff to hold their own authority and enabling them to develop their leadership capacity in a crisis, all the while knowing someone more senior is there to support them. Consider the risk of a prison leader behaving like an authoritarian parent towards less experienced staff. This must be all the more tempting in emergencies. In a prison environment, authoritarianism is a systemic risk, based on the perceived purpose of the organisation and how each prisoner arrived at this point in their life. Authoritarian compared to authoritative behaviour is something all staff, at any level of seniority, must endeavour to be especially conscious of. This recalls Phil's childhood experiences, how he was parented and neglected by his parents. And how a teacher – taking a parental role of sorts – inspired him to achieve a previously unimagined, positive, educational and professional outcome.

Prison leaders risk acting out authoritarian experiences they may have had earlier in their lives or careers. Alternatively, they may bring heightened awareness of the impact of such controlling or potentially abusive behaviours and consciously attempt to steer their and other's behaviour choices away from this.

Staying resilient

I return to the subject of resilience. From my observations of various clients and also time spent in the field, operating in challenging parts of the world, rest and relaxation is essential to remaining resilient. In many organisations where staff are required to deal with conflict, physical violence, psychological violence, fear and danger, for example in a medical, law and order, war reporting or a natural disaster context, respite is near impossible because it coincides with when the workload is at its most stressful and most urgent. Physical and psychological breaks are invariably delayed, sometimes multiple times. For logistical reasons, leaders often cannot afford to give themselves or anyone else time off. This is especially so in organisations where resources – financial, staffing and skills – are already stretched or being cut.

In my view, when it is possible to take time out, I believe it is essential for leaders to insist upon it, both for themselves and for their staff. This applies even if workers no longer think they need to rest. Adrenalised environments can become seductive.

Employees feel their work is vital, which it often is. They may not notice a depletion in their energy, compensating for it with snacking on sugar-loaded foods, drinking more alcohol, not exercising or, conversely, becoming hyperactive. Some people find they cannot rest. They cannot calm down. They are addicted to busy-ness. In this regard, leaders must develop a habit of gently monitoring those around them. Spotting people who deny their level of exhaustion, or who may be using work as a source of self-worth, identity or as an avoidance strategy for something going on at home, can be a useful informal barometer of psychological health.

I would advise proactively planning respite and opportunities to self-nurture ahead of time. For when the next crisis hits, there may not be time or mental 'bandwidth' to do this. People tip out of the other side of an emergency, feeling a mixture of exhilaration, success or sometimes failure. At first it can be difficult to focus on how to physically and emotionally refuel. Any trauma may be as yet unacknowledged or unaddressed.

Becoming practised at time-out behaviours helps leaders recover more quickly from particularly stressful episodes at work, boosting their medium and long-term resilience. Such conscious strategies attempt to avoid burn out, promoting organisational sustainability through keeping staff 'match fit' rather than running on empty. They are less likely to go on sick or resign.

Proactively developing and maintaining resilience in and around an immediate crisis is important, but leaders also need resilience to cope with the daily grind. This is the marathon of long-term exposure to challenging physical and psychological aspects of the job. This applies to work outside the prison context, including roles which require relentless amounts of travel, management across time zones, shift work, unpredictable hours or existential events. Senior leaders need the ability to keep going, whilst working long hours and dealing with complex projects or difficult people.

Reflecting on the role of a prison

Nowadays, command and control styles of behaviour are considered old fashioned and usually undesirable, except perhaps in specific urgent situations. Adopting a coaching style of leadership in an emergency may not be the best way to lead at all. There are times when being directive is a more appropriate choice.

So different, difficult leadership situations or contexts justify or even demand a range of flexibly deployed leadership styles. Those lower down the chain of command must consider when they risk taking up the role of 'parent' or 'child' at work. There are times when a person leads, times when they agree to follow, occasions when they fit in and adapt to others' requests or demands and times when they may refuse to do this. Some leaders become highly directional, controlling or even abusive, whilst others sink into a passive or even depressed looking stance. Building the capacity of managers to acknowledge their leanings and increase their self-knowledge in order to avoid potentially destructive behaviour choices tests senior leaders yet further.

Phil still thinks about the night when he had to remotely manage an outbreak of prison violence. His staff feared for their lives and then went on to ensure the safety of the very prisoners who were threatening to kill them:

> *The prison staff were incredibly brave. Flames were shooting everywhere. Prison officers were dragging prisoners out, giving them mouth to mouth. We could see the CCTV footage. The staff were resuscitating prisoners. The essence at this point is that it's life and death inside a prison.*

Consider the purpose of a prison. It is to lock people up. To segregate them from society in order, it is hoped, to ensure the safety of that society. Prisons play the role of demonstrating punishment and privation as a consequence for those who do not obey the law. Conceptually, prisons intend to be part of a functioning criminal justice system. They also have the potential to be part of a post-justice system, whereby prisoners rehabilitate and break their additive, destructive and sometimes highly lucrative but illegal behaviour patterns in favour of the straight and narrow path. Prisons can be educators of last resort, fielding young people who fell out of the school system or had traumatic upbringings which have contributed to them ending up 'inside'. No wonder Phil is so inspired by the potential of prisons and prisoners.

In practical terms, prisons are physical spaces which restrict freedom and refuse escape. They are secure containers for some of the less savoury characters in the community. In a riot situation, this secure container designed to make exit impossible for most of the people inside (staff excepted), is suddenly required to release its violent contents. For whilst the state has a duty to enable its citizens to live in safety, it also has a duty of care to protect those incarcerated in its prisons from harm. Translate that into an emergency situation where escape, sometimes from fire and smoke inhalation, is suddenly the imperative. It is like doing a handbrake turn: Spaces specifically designed to keep people in now need to be able to let them out, without compromising the wellbeing of wider society.

Leading in such an environment seems some distance from many management jobs where staff feel unsettled by a change of desk or a move to a different building. Plenty of leaders describe the challenges of steering a team through a complex project or an organisational restructure. What useful learning can be gleaned from the extremes encountered by leaders working in a prison context?

The hope of redemption

The word 'redemption', used in a prison context, is controversial. Its religious connotations can be considered inappropriate or patronising. Who has the right to decide if there is sufficient remorse and improvement, to allow redemption to occur? Phil believes in the hope of redemption. He thinks good prison management offers the possibility of both rehabilitation – disentangling oneself from the habit of repeat offending – and redemption, defined as saving or rescuing someone such that they can claim or reclaim a productive, non-criminal life.

Listening to Phil's accounts of prison life, I notice his energy, his drive, his commitment, his belief. A gentle compassion often seeps through his face as he speaks. At other times, it appears as if his skin has crumpled, like a scrunched-up ball of paper. As his coach, I offer my observation, as a fast track to what he is really thinking. Alongside the violence and fear he is exposed to in his job, Phil refuses to let go of his ambition that society must 'get prisons right', an ambition which is underpinned by his belief in the inherent goodness in most people. At a certain point, most inmates want to stop committing crime. At this time, they may need the greatest support, says Phil:

> *Some people believe prisoners are 'doomed to deviance'. They have mates who take drugs, parents who don't give a shit . . . their trajectory is like a train hurtling off the tracks, towards prison and you can't stop it. We've tried 'troubled families' interventions but it doesn't seem to make any difference.*

Whilst well-meaning interventions aimed at convincing inmates to go straight often do not work, it would appear that ageing does. There are patterns of offending. Young men in their early 20s start to belong to a crowd or a gang. They bond. It may be their first experience of feeling part of a family. Crime is integral to that sense of belonging. It is exciting, rewarding, lucrative; it brings status.

Prisoners have photos up in their cells of their flash cars, the women they are dating, the mother or mothers of their children. These men are wealthy. They feel rich. Financially speaking, they have serious money. Drug dealers can earn £5,000 a day. They are unlikely to be caught in the early years of their criminal activity, as they are not yet known to the police. Thieves can do burglary for some time and manage to stay under the radar.

Phil explained to me that as these men journey through their early 20s and into their late 20s, they start to see the younger men coming into prison. Suddenly they feel a bit old, as if life is passing them by. Turning 30 can be an epiphany. These men have a lot of money but they have spent a lot of time in prison, so they have not had much time to enjoy their wealth. By this stage offenders are known to the police, they are caught more frequently and earn longer prison sentences. Some men are in a stable relationship, with older children and a partner who decides they will not see their kids if they keep ending up in prison. At 30, a male prisoner starts to see himself as a 'family man'. His identity is now broader than just a prison identity number. At 35 these men want to change.

This point in a prisoner's life is a pivotal opportunity to launch the idea that they can break their cycle of crime. Some prisons run a family man course. Inmates are told that their children are two-thirds more likely to go to prison if they have a father who's 'done time'. Phil coaches them:

> *I say to them 'you are too old for this'. I tell them 'look at the youngsters coming in here . . . these people are idiots.' I become directive but not confrontational. You find a chink, where you can see them having doubts about their prison lifestyle. My role at that point is to offer hope.*

Identifying the tipping point at which an offender wants to change is vital. The next imperative is to offer them tools to tackle their drug problem, teach them to read and write, help them learn a trade or take a qualification. Each of these ingredients helps disrupt their need to commit crimes due to lack of employment, says Phil:

> *We need inmates to have lightbulb moments when they think they don't want 'this' to be their life. Ideally we need to make that realisation happen earlier and earlier. If you've had a series of 3-month sentences, next time you'll end up with a 4-year and then a 7-year sentence. If you can switch that cycle off early on – well, that's what I think my job is.*

Phil convinced some local companies to offer jobs to his prisoners whilst they were still in jail. It is part of generating hope and opportunity. He says he can tell a prospective employer more about his inmates than they would learn from reading the CV of a job seeker who walks in off the street. Phil knows what time his prisoners go to bed, what they have eaten for dinner. He has invested his trust in his prisoner's integrity and they know it.

Without a job and somewhere to live, leaving prison and living a conventional life can be almost impossible. Hence why the men in Phil's care are encouraged to create closer ties with their families. This is part of creating an upward spiral of self-belief, and a feeling that they are now making something of their lives begins. The sense of optimism and resolution is transmitted to me, even though I am not a prisoner and I did not coach Phil in a prison environment:

> *I do have doubts, but I'll also go to any length, take risks, spend money, bend the rules, trying to do the right thing – I'm on a mission to change the lives of the men in my care. None of my men have ever let me down. I never had a single failure, like a prisoner who went to work and didn't come back. It never happened. The chief inspector visited my prison and told me it was the best prison he'd ever been in. He said our prison should be a role model for other prisons to learn from. He said we'd demonstrated that excellence is possible. I thought 'blimey'!*

I asked Phil how his troubled family background influences or even enhances his ability as a leader, particularly in a prison context.

> *What I bring from my childhood, is empathy. I have an inherent belief in the goodness in the vast majority of people. I blamed my mother for my inability to cope with life events like splitting up with a girlfriend. . . . I knew my reactions were emotionally disproportionate to the way other people dealt with things. But I couldn't cope with the rejection.*

Phil's mother went to Alcoholics Anonymous for 20 years. Phil still occasionally attends Al-Anon, a support group for the families of and others affected by problem drinkers. His mother said:

Your problems might have my name on them, but the solutions have your name on them.

Phil found this acknowledgement empowering. His mother was telling him to sort his life out. When she suggested Phil attend Al-Anon meetings, it felt like the first bit of proper parenting she had ever given him. In turn, Phil's job offers him the opportunity to get a glimpse of 'proper parenting' for some prisoners, who may have had equivalently painful family histories to Phil's:

90% of prisoners in the UK come from dysfunctional backgrounds. Their parents may be alcoholics, they come from broken homes, their mates draw them into criminality. I know, because I was on the edge of that. I get where they're coming from. I also get that prisoners find excuses to not be the best they can be by blaming their parents, their circumstances or the police. I tell them what my mum said to me.

Phil believes in redemptive possibility. In rehabilitation over punishment. In helping criminals leave crime and cut cyclical behaviours of reoffending. He wants to rescue:

I like saving people. I felt 'saved'. Saved from a life of crime and feeling like a loser, by two remarkable teachers. As a result, my life ended up in place I never dreamt could be possible. I never imagined being so successful. I'm married, with a family, pets, family holidays. I could have ended up locked behind doors.

One of the thrills of Phil's job is meeting prisoners who have gone straight. He loves facilitating that journey:

One day I popped into a chemist in a small provincial town. A lad came up to me in his working gear. He was covered in mud and dirt. He said: 'Alright gov'? He was very friendly, but I wasn't sure which way this conversation would go. Then he said: 'I want to thank you for what you said to me that night on the wing. It made all the difference'. I didn't remember him, I didn't know his name, and I couldn't remember what I'd said. But in his head, something had sunk in.

The man in question was out of prison, living in the community, proud of and working hard at his job. Phil insists that all of us, including convicted (and arguably non-convicted) criminals, *can* choose the kind of person we want to be now, as well as the kind of person we want to become. Victor Frankl (Frankl 1984) argued that even in captivity – in his case being in the Auschwitz concentration camp during the second world war, where he was subjected to horrific physical and psychological suffering – a person always has a right to choose their attitude. Choice of attitude (Frankl is a freedom where there may be little freedom.

Despite Phil's determination to enlighten and help his prisoners, he is rooted in the realities of increasingly stretched resources, an overcrowded prison system and the rise in violence and suicide, both inside and outside prison:

> *I sometimes feel a dispirited leader. I manage an increasing amount of tension; an increasing number of men with an increasing number of issues. At the same time, we have to cut what we spend looking after them. It's incredibly difficult having to do that, as a leader. You feel disingenuous as know you're inflicting a kind of damage on people. I don't necessarily disagree with some of the systemic changes, but you still have to lead everyone through them.*

Once again, resilience is needed to deal with the dispiriting moments. The holding of both possibility and enthusiasm to improve the lives and potential of prisoners, along with the realities of budget cuts. Leaders across the public sector will no doubt identify strongly with this reality. Phil copes by expressing how fed up he feels, then being as imaginative and creative as he can be, with the money that he does have. Generating ideas is a constant thread in his leadership.

In his story, Phil shares much of what inspires and challenges him as a leader. There seems to be plenty Phil's prisoners can learn from him. But he has also learned from *them*:

> *I've learned that prisons and prisoners without hope are very dangerous places. If people spend many hours locked behind a door, with no opportunity to change, they'll become angry, frustrated and more likely to take drugs. Cycles of debt will arise as a result.*
>
> *I've learned that prisoners need to have something to lose. So, if they misbehave, that'll jeopardise the things that they want, like making a phone call to their wife, having a shower, being given access to training or an opportunity for a job. Why take drugs and end up with two weeks' solitary confinement when you could phone your family or play snooker with your mates in the wing? That's why I'm convinced about the redemption model of prison management. If prisoners are locked up all the time, they have nothing to lose. So, what I've learned is to make prisons places of incentives. Make them purposeful prisons. The governor must have a clear vision which seeks to engage prisoners in purposeful activities.*

The concept of meaning and purpose in a prison context has broader policy implications with potential benefit to civil society. If instead of cycling round a repetitive loop of reoffending and being locked up, criminals could choose to disrupt their destructive behaviour patterns to go straight and go to work – thus becoming economic contributors to society and positive role models to the next generation of children and young people, potentially preventing them entering a life of crime themselves.

Understand and be understood – applying learnings from prison leadership

I hinted earlier in this chapter about the potential to apply leadership learning from the prison environment to other fields of either commercial or public-sector work. I see common threads around authenticity and self-awareness. This includes the imperative for leaders to seek to understand themselves deeply, and to not be afraid of their limitations, yet know what they are. There is a risk that senior leaders are assumed to be experts because of their seniority. It is important that senior leaders do not collude with this assumption. Instead they have an opportunity to model honesty about their weaknesses or mistakes. This benefits their organisation, in terms of allowing swifter solutions to be sought earlier, when there is a problem. It also builds a culture of openness, humility and accurate self-assessment. Phil counsels this:

> *As a leader, never be unkind to those around you. You don't know what they may be struggling with, either inside or outside work.*

I find this statement immensely powerful. It travels with me because it can be applied in so many different contexts. Like some of the other leaders in this book, Phil used to be more directive than he is now. When he adopted a coaching approach to his conversations, he noticed that he became more successful and achieved better outcomes:

> *I was naturally directive. But nowadays I try to be myself, but with more skill. I borrowed that concept from Goffey and Jone's book entitled 'Why Should Anyone Be Led By You?' I can speak with the Secretary of State, a prison officer or an inmate on the prison landing. Inside my head I'm saying: 'Understand and be understood'. That's what I'd say to other leaders.*

Closing thoughts

This chapter has visited Phil's childhood roots, his route to education and his career working in prisons. He appears to have succeeded both despite and because of his childhood circumstances. He demonstrates an ability to deal with some of the toughest and most dangerous criminal gang members. Phil can reframe their behaviours through understanding the causes of them. He can deploy compassion when he sees an opportunity to rescue. Phil creates a vision for prisoners wanting to reintegrate back into society to be responsible partners and fathers. He enjoys facilitating their pathways forward, leaving their previous lives of crime. He helps them learn a skill and land a job.

Phil values what executive leadership coaching can bring leaders working in a prison context. Coaching is his sounding board. A place to externalise his thinking. Whilst extroverted leaders may speak in torrents as they work out their ideas, introverted leaders, who are more comfortable containing their thinking internally, also need a sounding board. It may take them more effort to use it. Most leaders at a senior level cannot openly express the full extent of their thinking because of confidentiality, market sensitivities or political considerations. So, the chance to talk, develop ideas and be psychologically 'held' by a highly present coach can make a significant contribution to wellbeing and success. It also offers challenge.

I would counsel coaches offering a sounding board to senior leaders to say little, be wholly present and give leaders silence in which to access and voice their inner process. Phil reflects:

> *Coaching is a chance to question your own expertise. It's important to have someone who is prepared to challenge you especially as you become more senior, because many people won't. Coaching must challenge a leader's internal assumptions and beliefs. I still remember my first coaching session with you when you asked: 'Is what you've just said a fact or an assumption'?*

Asking leaders what they are assuming, and for them in turn to ask their staff the same question, develops reflective and eventually reflexive thinking within the team. Phil continues to consider the assumption question. Recently, he explored his assumptions that doing his current job sets the rest of his working life, that because he works in prisons now he will always work in a prison environment. It was as if his career in prisons mirrored the beliefs his prisoners may hold about being stuck, locked in and unable to escape. Phil's self-limiting beliefs may reflect assumptions that inmates hold about why they've ended up in prison, how they are trapped in the system – be that the criminal justice system or the gang system. There appears to be no escape from their disadvantage. This is called parallel process.

It is interesting when leaders working in a particular environment, such as prisons, exhibit 'symptoms' or indicators which parallel the worries of their 'clients'. In the case of the men in Phil's care, their concerns about whether they will be released, or whether they will ever escape their life of crime. Assumptions can lock thinking into an inflexible place. Phil continues to be 'imprisoned' to some extent by his own upbringing. It is possibly no coincidence that his work environment is all about locking people up and securing or restricting their movement. At home growing up, there was nobody to 'contain' or 'hold' Phil emotionally or physically. As he sees it, it was a teacher who 'rescued' him. Now Phil consciously wants to save and rescue and repair. This is certainly an external intention. But it may also represent a continuation of the yearning for this for himself too.

Phil's assumption about being locked into a career in prisons contrasts his prisoners' assumption that he is a free man. When do leaders in other fields exhibit similarly imprisoned thinking, either due to professional or personal circumstances? What could these leaders be internalising, mirroring or representing about their organisations in how they think and behave?

This chapter paints a visual and at times visceral picture of life inside the male prison environment. The stories in one prison leader's narrative expose repeated cycles of destructive behaviour by prisoners, leading to debt, danger and feelings of despair. It explores crisis leadership, issues of authority and the potential to abuse control and power. The instances reveal how a small action can have an enormously significant and potentially life-changing result.

Leaders in such an environment must equip themselves with sufficient emotional insight, together with awareness of deliberate and inadvertent power mechanisms they or others may have in play. This can be at a conscious or unconscious level. Senior leaders need respite. They must recognise when they need to physically remove themselves from the prison environment in order to process their feelings.

For leaders in other disciplines – be it commercial or in the public sector – I think there is much to consider, in terms of imprisoned thinking, systemically representative behaviour, physical responses to fear and stress and for how with sufficient emotional support and reflection a disadvantage in the past can enhance rather than hold back a leader's success.

Leading behind bars: insights from inside. Leadership learning from a former prison governor who says in terms of crime, he could have 'gone either way'

Reflections for leaders

- Where could there be sub-cultures operating within your organisation?
- Who is *really* running your organisation then?
- Where might there be overt power?
- Where might you or your people have inadvertent power?
- Work mode: What circumstances in your role can cause you to 'split' off from your emotions?
- When might you as a leader be taking up the role of authoritarian parent?
- What have you learned about leading effectively, remotely?
- When was it easier to be directive, but not the right decision in leadership terms?
- When have you or a member of your team succeeded because of a difficulty in your past?
- When did you as a leader see an opportunity to offer hope?

Reflections for coaches

- Authority and power: Who might actually be in prison?
- When have leaders you coached taken up a 'parental' role and, if so, what type of parent did they become?

- If your client works in e.g. medicine, ask what part of them is sick

  e.g. humanitarian aid – ask if they need aid/rescuing
  e.g. start-up – ask what part of them they want to begin
  e.g. electronics – ask about connection, broken circuits, saturation

- Consider splitting as a defence against overwhelm
- Consider the potential in all of us, including leaders, to malfunction
- Integrate learning and consequences to break a pattern or cycle
- Where might elements in their past be holding them back from their full positive potential?
- What does the client bring from their childhood or an experience of disadvantage that could enhance rather than limit the quality of their leadership?

References

Frankl, V. (1984). *Man's Search for Meaning: An Introduction to Logotherapy*. New York: Touchstone (p. 75).

Freud, S. (1920). *Beyond the Pleasure Principle*. S.E., *18*: 7–64. London: Hogarth Press.

Kolb, D. A. (2015). *Experiential Learning: Experience as a Source of Learning and Development*. New Jersey: Pearson.

Menzies Lyth, I. (1960). Social systems as a defence against anxiety: An empirical study of the nursing service of a general hospital. *Human Relations*, 13, 95–121.

Suggested reading

Gerhardt, S. (2010). *The Selfish Society: How We All Forgot to Love One Another Made Money Instead*. London: Simon & Schuster (p. 71), ISBN 978-1-84739-676-1.

Gerhardt, S. (2014). *Why Love Matters: How Affection Shapes a Baby's Brain*. Hove: Brunner Routledge.

Goffee, R. and Jones, G. (2015). *Why Should Anyone be Led By You? What It Takes to be an Authentic Leader*. Boston: Harvard Business Review Press.

Chapter 7

Location location location

How one client claims his leadership learning was transformed, because of the different places, buildings and environments in which his coaching conversations took place

> *The breakfast area of the railway station hotel was a small, closed environment. For once, I was fully present in the space – I wasn't even thinking about work. I realised that I was about to board a train to where I grew up. I was literally moving my thinking to where lots of my ingrained work behaviours and internal thinking originated. I'm at a crossroads on my professional journey. But I have to sort out the personal journey.*

This is a story about walking and talking. It takes us to different London locations, from the Royal Festival Hall, to the National Portrait Gallery, the British Library and St James' Park. This chapter is about learning differently because we are thinking on our feet, or have changed location from the office, school or factory floor to a contrasting or different location. Often for logistical reasons, my clients are not able to find an available room to meet in their organisation's building. Or the coaching session in the room he or she did book keeps being interrupted by double bookings, the next booking or a colleague who has glimpsed us through the glass walls and waved. Increasingly, in my experience, coaching sessions have moved outside the workplace.

There are differing views on the importance and the impact of the location of learning. One view is that when we move around, we think anew. Another, in contrast, is that leaders wanting to learn how to be better leaders should learn in the environment where that learning needs to be applied. In other words, if you work in a factory, have your coaching sessions there and not in an office. If high performance in your job means achieving results on a race track, coach trackside. And if you need to deliver via multiple office-based or virtual teams, don't coach in a park. I see merit in both stances.

Some coaches work from consulting rooms. Others meet clients in their offices. After some discussion about what location suited best, I decided to take coaching outside the workplace – at first to an art gallery because it was raining, another time to a green open space, because it was dry. This evolved into a deliberately creative coaching approach. Clients liked it. They claimed they learned more. Some even say they can't think in the office. Consider what this could mean organisationally, in terms of innovation and productivity, if your employees believe that they cannot think effectively in their workplace environment.

This chapter on location presents a single, anonymised case study of a coaching client who evaluates the impact of coaching in a variety of mostly indoor venues in a busy capital city. The client, Jonny, reviews the experience of his peripatetic coaching programme. He agreed to be interviewed about his experiences of coaching in different locations some weeks after his coaching programme had ended. The chapter explores the potential psychological, reputational and subconscious risks being taken on both sides.

Location location location: how one client claims his leadership learning was transformed, because of the different places, buildings and environments in which his coaching conversations took place

> *If we'd stayed in my office building, I know I would only have revealed my work side. We would have talked about work issues. We would have remained stuck on work issues. I would have thought that all I could talk to you about were work issues. Changing locations meant that I no longer viewed you as a coach who could only help me with my current job, but one who would take a wider perspective to talk about personal things which affect me when I do my job.*

Jonny is a civil servant. He is married to an ambitious, career-focused engineer. They have a toddler. Jonny is passionate about books, art, history and his daughter's happiness. Jonny trained as a lawyer and then dipped into humanitarian aid before settling on his current government job. Any challenging, well-boundaried coach could have surfaced this client's deeper struggles around work and self-identity. However the different coaching locations in which we chose to meet served his learning in a more profound and meaningful way than had we met at his office.

Walking and talking or learning outside in the open air is hardly a new concept. The Greek philosopher and teacher Aristotle (384–322 BCE) was given to walking about whilst he lectured. The word 'peripatetic' is derived from the ancient Greek word peripatetikos, meaning 'walking about' or 'given to walking', effectively learning 'al fresco'. It is thought that Aristotle's peripatetic stance derives from his lack of status in Athens. Non-citizens could not own property. So, Aristotle and others convened meetings outdoors and in public spaces.

I believe that change or motion or 'place' influences how we think and behave in relation to an event or challenge. My decision to use interesting public spaces, including outdoor spaces, for coaching was partly a practical solution to needing somewhere to coach near my client's place of work. Hence my desire to find free spaces in a city rich with cultural stimulation. This practical solution is now integrated in my coaching philosophy: Creativity, depth and emotional self-analysis, using visual cues, place or environment as a stimulus. This is a nod to neuroscientific findings about the influence of movement on thinking. Plus, working with the environment, including occasional distractions or noise, not despite it, I regard as an embodiment of a systemic or constellations approach in coaching (Whittington 2016).

Whilst much of my practice is underpinned by psychoanalytic thinking, professional coaches are not obliged to see clients in the same 'treatment room' as might a therapist. Therapy rooms are meant to be neutral, stable spaces, so that the client can't avoid 'the work'. The constant location a therapist offers their client gives a sense of the rules. It is not exciting; the focus is solely on the work. But this private space, shut away from the wider world, risks being inappropriately intimate.

Another risk of a consultation room is that the space may also 'represent' the therapist or coach – showing off the number of journals they have read or the artworks they own; the location may even communicate or seek to communicate, an impression of how successful the practitioner is and how much they earn.

Meeting a client in a public space means the coach is less reliant on having an impressive office or consultation room. There is no window dressing of the coach. This shifts the power dynamic back to the client. It is not the coach's turf. Nor the clients' territory. It is neutral. Unless of course the coach is an expert in the art or the architecture of the building, in which case the supposedly neutral territory subconsciously represents a power play by the coach for dominance over the client. Similarly, should the client hold expert knowledge, the power arrangement can reverse.

Public spaces as a concept protect both client and coach, from 'too much intimacy'. But then the concern is whether the chosen location creates avoidance of deeper work by the client, because the environment is so interesting. An art gallery or a green open space risks rescuing the client and/or the coach from tackling the difficult issues. There is also the risk of developing intimacy if the enjoyment of the location becomes the focus. But if the location is used to demand more depth of thinking from the client, it is serving the work or even enhancing the quality of outcome from the coaching.

Without careful, conscious management, the downloading of knowledge which is unrelated to the coaching goals can deflect from the very work required of the client, as the coach becomes in awe of or intellectually stimulated by the client's cultural repertoire. Paintings and sculptures risk becoming props, potentially masking poor quality coaching, or colluding in a strategy of avoidance through distraction and deflection by the client, of work issues they would rather not address. Stimulating locations may also challenge a coach to work more creatively and organically, whilst retaining focus on a leader's development goals. The coach must manage the potential for power and dominance by either party, subconsciously or otherwise, in the choice of location and the nature of the conversation which evolves within it, to protect the genuineness of the coaching process.

> *'I had never considered the context,'* says Jonny. *'The location, the surroundings – and of the impact of where we coached, would have in terms of what I learned and the thinking that I had as a result. I was inhibited by my work. I was closed, low energy, I felt bad about myself. I conformed. Because I took the mental image of my office building, a beautifully restored old building, conveying history, solidity and long-term endurance, into the wider world, I limited the scope of what I thought I could do at work.'*

The Royal Festival Hall – coaching session 1

This relaxed lounge, above a concert venue on the banks of the River Thames in London, England, provides an informal, albeit public place, for people to have meetings. This was the first coaching session. It carried a sense of sounding out for both coach and client, of how the coaching relationship would work. There can be resistance and nervousness on both sides as rapport is attempted, and the coaching gets going and establishes a momentum.

Jonny described how this 1950s building didn't mean anything to him. That is because its *mental location* (Armstrong 2005) continues to represent the office. Jonny says that because I had brought with me some pictures of art, this managed to bring him out of himself.

Before coaching, Jonny seemed to be 'splitting' (Klein 1975). A work persona, a home persona, a parent persona, a laddish persona. The client expended energy working against himself, as his various personas competed against one another. He could not seem to integrate who he was successfully. One might read into his feedback on the location a mixture of honesty in reflection and rejection towards the coach – perhaps, also, fear.

Charing Cross Hotel Breakfast Room – coaching session 2

The next coaching session, a month later, was at the Charing Cross Hotel Breakfast Room. This was a last-minute rearrangement requested by Jonny when his father was suddenly taken ill and admitted to hospital. Jonny was to take a train, directly following our meeting, to see him. Charing Cross Station is symbolic of a cross-roads. Jonny was cross with his alcoholic father for self-damaging behaviour which led to him being in hospital yet again. Cross-roads suggests a choice of options or directions. The location of a station also offered Jonny a direct route out of the coaching session, should one be needed, poised for a journey towards his relative, home, roots and childhood. I reflected on the notion of meeting in a hotel: The word 'hotel' can have an association with the illicit; for business people, a hotel offers a place to have a tax-efficient coffee. (In the UK many business meetings take place in hotel lobbies rather than cafes, for this reason.)

The breakfast area was a small, closed environment, which allowed Jonny to open up more about personal things which he reflected on in that meeting:

> *I'm at a crossroads on my professional journey. But I needed to sort out the personal journey. For once, I was fully present in the space – I wasn't even thinking about work. . . . I realised that I was about to board a train and literally move my thinking to the town where I grew up.*

Or rather, the town in which he had failed to 'grow up'.

Jonny had made the connection between some of his ingrained, repetitive and almost compulsively destructive work behaviours and the potential for them to have foundations in his family experiences as a young boy. He was moving to the scene of where much of his rebellious thinking originated. Maybe he was at a cross-, i.e. a being cross, roads.

> *If we had met at my office, every session would have confirmed that I can't change . . . it's about literally stepping out of the building . . . such that you*

> *can see multiple perspectives and a wider view of all sorts of career options, ideas and solutions.*

The National Portrait Gallery – coaching session 3

At the end of our previous meeting Jonny said:

> *I'm all about people. That's what I care about as a leader. Let's meet at the National Portrait Gallery.*

He did not turn up. It was the client's choice of location. And the client's choice not to turn up. Jonny subsequently invested considerable energy – including trying to contact me over the weekend – apologising and trying to pay me directly himself rather than letting his organisation pick up the tab. He blamed lack of self-organisation.

> *I'm sorry, I feel awful. I'm always doing this . . . I need to get a personal assistant to manage my diary. It won't happen again.*

There seemed to be genuine remorse but also a boyish charm at play. A repeated pattern revealed. And not much to indicate anything might change it. This was merely another surface symptom, where I suspected something deeper was playing out.

Jonny insisted that this was an important aspect of the coaching relationship and that it deserved attention. I should not skim over this incident and 'rescue' him from embarrassment or exposure. I agreed. It presented us with a richness of data to explore. Was it simply a mishap, given that in previous coaching sessions Jonny had turned up on time and in the right place? He could have been avoiding or escaping from having to deal with something he knew was important. He may have feared I had seen through him and would land on an issue he did not want to face. He may have been hoping to be caught; wanting me to see his destructive, repetitive pattern of letting people down. He may have been taking control. Seeking power over me, perhaps because in his eyes I held too much power. I also wondered if, given that I was about 10 years older than him, Jonny cast me as his mother or a headmistress to his naughty school boy role. Either way, I did not want to collude with his behaviour.

> *'That no-show session was terrible,'* says Jonny. *'It's about having an adaptive, self-absorbed personality. You held the boundary and absolutely didn't collude.'*

Perhaps Jonny found his choice of a large, white-walled gallery space insufficiently containing. His statement about self-absorption possibly represents the behaviour of his substance-abusing father, rather than his own behaviour.

I consciously chose not to placate by saying: *'It's OK, don't worry . . . we can reschedule'*. Instead I said nothing. I let him talk. I kept it dispassionate and practical. I asked him what he thought his no-show was about. I asked him to reflect on the value of coaching for him. Or the value of his coach for him. I asked him to reflect on whether in fact he did not want the session despite saying that he did. I wondered if we scheduled another session whether he intended to turn up.

Jonny offered these reflections on his behaviour:

> *You have to lead by your actions. Being a boy versus taking responsibility for the effect you have on other people's lives. Missing that session was a wakeup call: 'Why am I massively disorganised? What feeds this? I keep getting away with letting people down. I can't continue to live, hoping and wanting and needing to be liked.'*

It is interesting that the client linked his need to be wanted and liked with behaviour patterns that can have exactly the opposite effect. Subconsciously the client may actually need or want to be punished rather than liked. He has offered me exposure to his inner world. One should not ignore such an invitation to notice rather than ignore his actions. So, it appears that Jonny sets up behaviours to ensure this happens.

There are many work and home situations where 'unconscious enactment' occurs. This refers to behaviours, in this case, between leader and coach, whereby both sides project unconscious meaning onto each other or a mutual situation. So, the coach may feel rejected – tapping into issues the coach may hold in their past, connected to rejection or inclusion. Equally, the client, in this case the leader who is doing the rejecting by not turning up, may be projecting quite another set of behaviours onto the situation. This mutual emotional ping-pong may be difficult to disentangle. But both sides must watch out for if it is going on.

I note Jonny's name. Jonny. Not Jonathan, which is the full adult name but the shortened version, often associated with childhood. I reflect on this client's choice of name in introducing himself, considering whether it connects with his laddish, childlike stance which to some extent, this client says, he refuses to abandon.

The point here is about having the playful creativity to notice, question and be prepared to let go of any hypothesis generated. In Coaching Supervision, I am challenged to approach each coaching conversation 'free of memory and desire' (Bion 1963). I ask leaders seeking to uphold a coaching culture at work to approach meetings, appraisals and tricky or confrontational conversations similarly.

Jonny reports that his coaching journey had seen him grown up. He claims that he has shifted from his previously boyish self-image to being a more authentic leader. Colleagues started to notice his more informal style of dress at work. Jonny now interrupts and challenges, rather than adaptively agreeing to whatever everyone else says. He makes jokes in meetings, which are increasingly appreciated as an addition to his leadership. Before coaching, Jonny thought he had to wear a suit and be serious. He was playing a part. He was not being true to himself.

The National Portrait Gallery – coaching session 4

There was a poignancy to meeting here after the previous failed attempt. Non-avoidance of this location was deliberate on both sides. When we met, Jonny made it clear that he was very invested in developing new processes to become more organised. But he quickly got rid of his PA:

> *I realised that's outsourcing the problem. It's outsourcing my responsibility.*

As we walked around the gallery, Jonny said the paintings helped him explore the unexpected; themes he hadn't thought to bring to the coaching session emerged:

> *It's about a journey through history . . . different paintings from different eras, representing things like domestic entanglement, growing up, other people's journeys, the passing of time, circles of human history, other people's worlds.*

I reflected at that point whether the paintings stimulated a clear articulation of themes my client knew he needed to work through; it may have been easier to look at a painting rather than the coach. Jonny continued his analysis of the coaching session in the art gallery:

> *It's like the grief curve*[1]*you showed me . . . the pictures provoked in me that I wanted to change. The varied locations are like being down in the mush . . . the depression, the confusion at the bottom of the curve. I'm asking how I get out of the low?' To which I replied: 'How do you think you can get out of the low?'*

The National Gallery – coaching session 5

Some of the pictures, marble columns, grand hallways and mosaic-tiled floors provoked a negative, almost repulsed reaction from my client:

> *The building itself is not powerful for me. Those Canaletto paintings of Venice are copies of the real thing . . . I'd rather see people and emotions. For me, a building is just a depository for what's inside – the contents and the stories.*

Perhaps the client feels himself to be like a copy of the 'real thing'. Picking up on his use of the word 'depository', Jonny may be using the building as a vessel for his self-disgust. His dislike of the building may represent his dislike of himself.

I asked Jonny why he had chosen to conduct his coaching in this space. Once again, it was for him about the value of doing some thinking, outside what he saw as the confines of his office building. He then happened upon an enormous painting of a lion with a small dog at its heels:

> *The lion is never tamed, it's wild. It shows it's pointless trying to fight nature. The dog is domesticated. That's what people want to do to each other. I*

needed to find out that my occasionally 'wild' or rebellious behaviours don't work. They don't allow me to escape feeling trapped.

Jonny is referring to feeling trapped by his job, his role, the expectations others may have of his career, or by his wife who may be attempting to domesticate or train Jonny.

This is an indication that the client is saying he will not change, is not willing to change or believes he cannot change. His laddish persona has too strong a draw for him. Or it is a reaction against the pull from his highly organised wife to be sensible and grown up. What the client felt, saw and where he was standing during a coaching session seemed to elicit almost instant reflective depth, self-reveal and clarity.

I analysed whether the dog was a representation of myself, the coach. I might have been led, strung along. Maybe I am being dominated by the inevitably stronger lion. Or the reverse, perhaps the client perceives me on a subconscious level as the lion – the one holding all the power, whilst he internally feels chaotic and not in control. This could also be why the client needs to recast me as the dog. This teenage, rebellious client with his laddish, immature side, may resemble to himself not the roaring lion, but rather the chained dog.

On discussing this case study with a group of psychoanalytic colleagues, a strong reaction to Jonny's choice of painting emerged. One version was that I am the dog and he is the lion. That the client will not make real shifts in his behaviour however much he tells me that he is changing. There is a suspicion that the client's version of his story – that of having a wild side – is in fact the reverse: That he doesn't have a wild side. Instead he is passive and impulsive. Jonny wants someone to treat him differently – i.e. for his coach to name this and not let him get away with his patterns and excuses.

We should consider also, the choice of language used by leaders and coaching clients. For example, Jonny talks about his 'wild side'. It may be more glamorous to represent this as exciting and powerful rather than infantile, impulsive or lacking in potency over his behaviours.

Whilst the dog on a leash may push and pull its owner all over the place, so too can a coaching client who tries to please whilst also trying to rebel. Those working with this person – or maybe you are this person – risk provoking others to fulfil a range of responses which may damage others, damage self or serve to play into and maintain destructive behaviour patterns. For example, forgiving, excusing, chastising, becoming angry or annoyed. Parenting or protecting or going into victim mode. Those involved must refuse to become caught up in this dance. Such psychological arrangements risk becoming seductive without others realising they have become entangled or that they are being 'played' with.

There is much for leaders of others, and coaches working to support those leaders, to hold in mind, to control the impulse to collude, for example, whilst simultaneously concentrating on the surface conversation.

We continue the coaching journey: As well as portraits, art and history, Jonny loves books. We arranged the next coaching session at the British Library.

The British Library – coaching session 6

The 'Treasures Room' of the British Library in London features a string of modern to ancient artefacts from various disciplines: Maps, musical compositions, novel extracts, botanical illustrations, tracts of Shakespeare and religious texts. Jonny finds relaxation and escape through books. But this location (as with other locations such as the Royal Festival Hall and the National Gallery), did not work for Jonny, who reacted strongly to finding thousands of volumes stored behind glass. He observes the space:

> *You can't touch these books. Books shouldn't be like that. I can see banks of university students on laptops, all plugged into their music. It's like a massive social experiment! Nobody is even reading a book!*

They may not have appeared to be reading a book, but with today's digital libraries and online access to academia, the students may have been reading intently. This is about the interpretation this leader gave to what he saw, or indeed what he was looking for in others. Within the negative resonance of this location, Jonny found a positive personal clarity:

> *I realise I don't want to work in a subdued, dark, untouchable environment. I want to be creative.*

Jonny doesn't like the building. Rather than his observations being solely an architectural response, he may be, as we saw with the National Gallery, projecting a dislike of himself, into the space itself, or indeed the 'coaching space'.

I offer Jonny another interpretation, that the 'architectural' response represents a disappointment with his own internal architecture. Aspects of himself he feels are poorly designed, not well executed, or that he wishes took a different form. There may be spaces he cannot access, either consciously or subconsciously. The walled off books are tomes so old they need to be protected in specially acclimatised conditions; the hostility displayed in relation to this situation represents a possible desire for access to a womb-like state that one cannot have in the British Library, nor in other areas of life, without prior permission.

Jonny's reaction could signal a frustrated desire for intimacy, including possibly sex with his coach. Or somebody else who is not available, interested or accessible to him.

Given an age difference between us, I had considered the possibility of being cast by the client in a maternal role, rather than as a sexually desirable object. In both cases our task as coach is to be alert to the possibility of conscious or subconscious projections of a sexual nature. Some leaders and coaches find the notion of sexual transference or sexual projection uncomfortable. We may not welcome them. But it may still be going on. Be that from the client or from the coach. Or between a leader and their direct reports.

It is one thing for a leader to hold awareness of the unsaid or for a coach to access a narrative for the subconscious, but another to voice it. Not everything that has been noticed needs to be mentioned. But it is important to search for the subconscious at play.

Aware of the potential for sexual undercurrents of a walking and talking meeting, albeit one without any body contact, I deliberately retain my usual pen and paper for making notes. I am signalling to the client and to any onlookers that our strolling around an art gallery is a business meeting, not a date.

St James' Park – our last meeting

Jonny's coaching programme took place during a dreary, rainy winter in the UK. Thus it was confined to mainly indoor locations which were near his office or his commute home. The interview for this case study however hit on a glorious, sunny day which took us to our last location: St James' Park.

> *Here there is a breeze blowing, there's a pond, there are pelicans, there are employees walking by . . . lots of careers, strolling along. That's how I see my next job – comfortable, unconfined, an open space. I'm more comfortable with a wide perspective now. You've moved me from a place of being a chained-up dog, concerned only with my work persona . . . to be a whole person. I can now add value as myself. I have a more confident stance. I achieve more in a work day and turn up at home a better person.*

Jonny is referring to becoming more reliable, ceasing to repeat destructive patterns such as 'forgetting' appointments or being late and cycling round his learned behaviours of charm and apology in a possibly compulsive repetition of negative behaviours. Jonny claims also that he is better aligned with himself as an adult and, thus, his internal struggle between being a 'bit of a lad' and his role of responsible father and mature employee has calmed somewhat. He claims to be conscious of deeper emotional triggers, responding more appropriately now compared to before he experienced executive leadership coaching. Jonny feels more authentic to himself and therefore more comfortable as a leader.

Jonny believes coaching helped him out of the self-destructive mush, towards a clearer path. He is now more open to not knowing. Any job move he considers will be underpinned by a conscious awareness of his main strengths, interests and wholeness as a person. He is listening to what he enjoys. He is also listening to changes in his energy, as data for what he cares about and what he doesn't. As an outcome of coaching he resists fulfilling the expected behaviours people may have had of him. He accepts himself and feels more genuine for it.

The same could have been achieved by conventional coaching sessions, meeting in one place. But Jonny argues otherwise:

> *If we'd had 6 coaching sessions in my work building, it would have been more tools and techniques-based. [He means transactional rather than transformational coaching.] You wouldn't have been able to get the same stuff out of me. So, I wouldn't have made the same depth of progress. I probably would not have actually engaged properly in the coaching process at all.*

But this might not be the case. I am aware that Jonny knows what to say to flatter or please me. A coach must not be seduced by flattery, but rather question it. Jonny may be creating a positive ending to our relationship. Or he may fear informing me that we have 'failed' to improve him. Jonny may believe that he has achieved behaviour shifts. I coach every client with the intention to create sustained outcomes – lasting change and consciousness which endures beyond the end of their coaching programme.

Closing thoughts

There is a lot to think about whilst appearing to walk and talk with ease of listening. There can be considerable professional reputational risk as well as the potential for unintended psychological consequences.

For example, outside of the usual business context, the client may share issues with their coach that they have not even shared with their partner. Such authenticity is welcomed on one level. It is often a fundamental part of many coaching interventions with leaders. However, the coach's supportive stance may be interpreted at a subconscious level as 'incoming love'. The client may then want to reciprocate that 'love' in some away.

Jonny claims that coaching brought him significant success and that the experience of learning in a variety of locations helped him as a leader. Yet exploring this case study with a group of psychoanalysts resulted in a brutal consensus: Jonny has not changed at all.

But their negative assessment must also be questioned. It could represent resistance from the psychological community to my working 'on location' in this way. There might also be envy of what some of them term my creative application of psychoanalytic principles, whilst not being formally trained as a psychoanalyst.

The point about sexual transference of the client's unconscious desires could be valid or invalid. What was unsaid in the professional group discussion was whether it represented not the client's desires, but some of the analysts' transference of their desires onto me.

Offices and organisations are systems of power, desire and envy. Leaders need to at least attempt to think about transferences they may emit, or become caught up in. After all, none of us is uncontaminated nor impossible to contaminate. This is about known knowns and known unknowns. It is about holding in mind processes which we may not intend or even realise are going on. The task of leaders and coaches supporting leaders who are growing is to learn what to ask, to learn to inquire. To master the notion of introducing ourselves to thinking about the unconscious at work.

Jonny claims that coaching on location helped him quickly dive deeper. He claims the inner results – which he claims are visible to colleagues – are profound for him and anchored in self-awareness and commitment. They seemed to release him from the rebellious reflexes generated by feelings of being trapped in the office. Or the perception of being trapped in other parts of his life.

Acknowledging the ethical and subconscious risks of working in a variety of coaching locations – such as subconscious notions of power, money, even sex – I believe that coaching on location can help the client's thinking and personal development. Their professional performance is bound to benefit. But the coach must remain acutely aware of whether the location is adding and deepening the work, or whether it is a distracting prop. A prop which risks the coaching conversation sinking into an avoidant friendship or worse, something akin to a 'date'.

The reality might be a mid-point whereby the client has shifted and self-improved but perhaps not to the enduring extent they predict. There is the risk of the client convincing themselves of deep change, believing that they have convinced their coach of this too. It makes for a more comfortable 'ending' between the two parties.

A coach must be sufficiently psychologically grounded, to honestly appraise whether they have succeeded or failed to help a client. This is partly about the adequacy of the coaching but also about recognising when the work issues presented hook into deeper issues which require psychotherapy, not coaching. In Jonny's case, I suspect that any change was not real, or if it was, not sustained. The deeper journey may be about Jonny's plea of intention to change. Thus intention is the work, rather than achieving changes on the surface.

I believe, in this leader's case, that the locations added metaphor, represented ideas for him or threw up important visceral reactions and connections; they helped him articulate deep-seated patterns of behaviour and thinking, which he then attempted to address. Whether his claimed changes endured, or were even true in the first place, we may never know.

Location location location: how one client claims his leadership learning was transformed, because of the different places, buildings and environments in which his coaching conversations took place

Reflections for leaders

- What spaces or locations do you work in and what is their impact on your thinking?
- What is their impact on your behaviour?

- Imagining the painting of the lion and the chained dog: What could this mean for you?
- Are you the dog or the lion?
- What does a chain symbolise for you?
- What transference could be going on – sexual or otherwise – between you and those you lead?
- If you are being coached 'on location', what is the impact of the choice of venue on your learning?
- What locations enable your best thinking and which do not?

Reflections for coaches

- Location as a prop, convenient meeting place or distraction from the real issue at hand
- The practicalities of taking notes if you're walking and talking – this could test your ability to stay wholly present, listen with ease and take notes or not take notes (Kline 2015*)
- Coaching *with* the location, not despite the location – dealing with noise and unexpected distractions
- How does the chosen location benefit this leader's learning?
- Whose territory are you on?
- Transference – what could be going on beneath the surface level of the coaching conversation?

Note

1 E. Kubler Ross. (2014). *On Death and Dying: What the Dying Have to Teach Doctors, Nurses, Clergy and their Own Families*. New York: Scribner.

References

Armstrong, D. (2005). *Organisation in the Mind: Psychoanalysis, Group Relations and Organisational Consultancy*. (Chapter 1, p. 4). London: Karnac.

Bion, W. R. (1963). *Elements of Psychoanalysis*. New York: Basic Books.

Klein, M. (1975). *Envy and Gratitude: And Other Works 1946–1963*. London: Random House.

Kline, N. (2015*). *More Time to Think: The Power of Independent Thinking*. London: Hachette.

Kubler-Ross, E. (2014). *On Death and Dying: What the Dying Have to Teach Nurses, Doctors, Clergy and their Own Families*. New York: Scribner.

Whittington, J. (2016). *Systemic Constellations: The Principles, Practices and Applications for Individuals, Teams and Groups*. London: Kogan Page.

Chapter 8

Desires and defences

Leadership in a refugee context

> *I am 58 years old. I'm becoming an elder. I look back at my life and wonder what I have learned and where I can be most useful. I would like to give my knowledge to somebody else otherwise I will take it with me to my grave. That doesn't seem very efficient. You become more and more experienced in life and then you stop work and that's it.*

In this chapter we draw on three case studies: Claudia, Holly and Noori. Claudia, an experienced leader working in a refugee context in Syria and Iraq. Holly, a young volunteer who distributed blankets and saucepans in refugee camps in France and Greece and Noori about what it is like for a host community in Pakistan to experience a sudden influx of refugees. The three women's testimonies explore the concepts of desires and defences applied to the refugee context. Their exploration includes themes such as neutrality, attachment and attack; shelter, abandonment, the transmission of trauma, eldership, endings and loss.

Desires and defences: leadership in a refugee context

The United Nations defines a refugee as someone who:

> *is forced to flee his or her country because of persecution, war, or violence. A refugee has a well-founded fear of persecution for reasons of race, religion, nationality, political opinion or membership in of a particular social group. Most likely they cannot return home or are afraid to do so. War and ethnic, tribal and religious violence are leading causes of refugees fleeing their countries.*
>
> [www.unrefugees.org]

In other words, refugees have fled terror and crossed an international border. In Syria and Iraq hundreds of thousands of people have fled civil war. But many of them have not crossed an international border. They seek safety and refuge in their own country. As Internally Displaced People (IDPs), they do not qualify for refugee status and the legal provisions which go with it. Yet their needs are often identical.

The refugee context evokes a cascade of desires and defences: *Desires* can be physical, emotional, political or spiritual. Refugees desire to escape from danger and trauma, seeking instead safety and protection. Onlookers may wish to help, offering shelter, hospitality and hope, either informally or as volunteers or donors to official aid agencies. Desires can become entangled. Local people wishing to alleviate the suffering of others may simultaneously fear losing out to the new arrivals. Some may want insulation from the threat posed by an influx of people, in terms of employment and housing. Those living or working in a refugee environment desire protection from the effects of another's trauma.

This leads us to think about the *defences* operating in a refugee context. Trust, fear, barriers, segregation (voluntary or otherwise), protectionist mafias, little businesses which spring up within or nearby refugee camps.

Few people *want* to become refugees or IDPs. Sensitivity must be given to their need as human beings, to honour certain cultural traditions such as generosity and hospitality. Even in desperate situations, people still need dignity. This applies in individual interactions as well as to systemic frameworks designed to help refugee populations.

It would be naive to omit a reality that the refugee context also presents opportunities to make money. There are multi-million-dollar contracts to win, ongoing deals of constructed (i.e. unnecessary) dependency and corruption going on behind the scenes. Not everybody has a desire to help alleviate suffering. For some, the longer a war goes on, the higher the rewards. It would also be naive to assume all refugees are genuine. Many are not refugees at all, but economic migrants, often young men, sent ahead by their families in search of a better life in another country.

The senior leader in a refugee context

> *The most genuine indicator of a person's leadership you'll find is by asking those who are led by that person.*

Claudia is known as the soul of her organisation. Her team says she is a great communicator. She is accessible and regards every individual, from the office driver upwards, as a valued *person.* As a leader, Claudia attempts to create an enabling environment in which she says those who know much more than she does can flourish and succeed.

Claudia believes that when people feel they are devising strategies and making decisions, they stop looking at the organisation as their employer, but rather as an extension of their vision, their dreams, their interests:

> *Then you have them on the hook and they really develop!*

A former mechanical engineer, born in Germany, Claudia has dedicated much of her working life to helping others. She has worked with refugees and internally displaced people in Syria, Iraq and Palestine, in Kenya, Sudan and Guatemala. In Claudia's international non-governmental organisation, teams cross refer. They exchange information about what they are doing and what they need. People help each other:

> *There is a temptation to have each department doing its particular job. I want people to talk to each other. We have weekly white-board meetings to show everyone what we're all doing. It works really well because at some point, instead of silo working, people start doing the connecting questions themselves.*

Claudia leads such that her direct reports learn to lead each other. She offers a shepherding or parenting of sorts, with encouragement to collaborate and self-solve independently. I talk to Claudia in her noticeably pristine, white-walled office in Damascus, Syria. Her usual working environment, however, can be far from clean and orderly. Instead it is fraught with physical and emotional destruction.

On a trip to a series of Syrian camps for internally displaced people, Claudia found, just as she had seen in Iraq, thousands of people living outside the official camp. Inside the camp, which contained 32 thousand people, there were neat rows of tents, shower blocks and even a market for fruit and vegetables and household goods. The camp was full. Eight thousand people were living outside its walls, in their cars and in makeshift shelters. Here there was no sanitation, no access to clean water and no garbage collection; open defecation increased the risk and spread of serious diseases. The perceived lack of modesty for women and girls contributed further to this risk: Many women waited until night time to relieve themselves or used a bucket kept in the corner of their tent, emptying it under cover of darkness.

In such conditions, there is physical suffering. But there is also mental suffering. Those lucky enough to make it into the official refugee camps then find they are not allowed to leave them. That is because of the threat of ISIS [the organisation which terms itself the Islamic State of Iraq and the Levant] infiltration, i.e. people pretending to be refugees but in fact planning to attack those inside the camp.

Genuine refugees – I use the term refugee here colloquially, to mean someone who is seeking refuge from danger, rather than the official UN definition which excludes internally displaced people – become frustrated. They feel they have escaped danger only to find their freedom to visit relatives or even go to the doctor is taken away from them. Such infantilisation – the return of an adult to a childlike state or status – is the price of trying to make camps secure places of refuge. In some camps, mini-businesses spring up, such as taking bribes for an exit pass or overcharging for a SIM card. At every turn, people can be seen responding and adapting to their situation.

When asked the 'miracle question', used in Solution Focus coaching, to elicit greater imagination and shunt people out of 'stuck', all people asked for was soap and tents. The camp managers were saddened by how little such desperate people said they wanted. Many refugees have never actually been asked what they need. Refugee agencies decide for them. Some refugees are no longer used to thinking.

Honouring Claudia's belief that humanity and dialogue lie at the heart of working usefully with refugees or internally displaced people, she set up a focus group consultation to evaluate the hygiene kits given out to people arriving at the camps. Girls rated the black plastic garbage bag as the most important – above toothbrushes and soap. Older women said soap and washing powder were the most important items. This is why . . .

For girls, the embarrassment of menstruating created feelings of unbearable exposure. They valued the black bag, because this meant they could discreetly dispose of soiled sanitary towels. Married mothers felt similarly, but for them soap and laundry powder were even more important because much of their day was spent cleaning and washing the family's clothes.

A significant proportion of girls and women avoid the public shower blocks. Or they go with other girls as 'bee keepers', who stand guard. Someone peeping through a hole in the wall and seeing a naked girl or woman can feel like a catastrophic violation in Arabic culture. In response to this, fathers and brothers busy themselves using their ingenuity to curtain off a bit of tent, create a sand or concrete floor and push a piece of piping underneath it, to drain the water. Thus the women have a private 'en-suite' shower, instead of having to use a public space to wash.

It may appear that refugees with no jobs, no school and no homes to keep have nothing to do all day. But it is quite the opposite. Women are overworked: Cooking, cleaning, standing in food queues within the refugee camp and taking care of their children. There is no respite, no hour in the week when they are childfree. Men occupy themselves building shelters and trying to arrange money, employment, contacts and paperwork, hoping to take their families on elsewhere. Compared to some refugee groups, Syrians are highly educated and highly motivated. They have much to contribute to the workforce of a new host country.

Life inside a refugee camp is hard enough. But those living outside it fare worse, living in disused or unfinished buildings, abandoned supermarkets and old petrol stations, which have no lighting, no windows or doors, no bathrooms. There isn't enough water to wash cooking pots. Everything is covered in flies. People don't eat well, they don't sleep well and they can't keep themselves clean. Children have no structure or stimulation. Boys, in particular, act out the trauma they have experienced by playing increasingly aggressive games. The long-term effects of such play and the inner anger which accompanies it are likely to present yet more challenges as time goes on.

Because these people don't live in officially designated refugee or even IDP camps, the various agencies bringing help to the region have no obligation nor resources to assist. Thus, the informally displaced can be even more vulnerable.

Their healthcare needs may be even greater than for those living in official refugee camps, as the poor, sick and elderly venture just a few kilometres outside of conflict or famine zones. There are no psychological services. Everywhere there is grief, despair, indignity and loss of hope.

There is also corruption. Some local authorities in Iraq, for example, use the official IDP camps as a financial opportunity. Contracts are awarded to cousins. A decision to truck water into the camp, rather than building a piped water supply, is underpinned by the desire to create an ongoing source of income, rather than giving best value for money. This is the 'war economy'. Multiple motivations, desires and defences are engaged. It is an assumption to think there is universality in the desire for peace. There are profits to be had from misery and potentially even more money to be made from inefficiency.

Claudia is not naive to this. She is equally troubled by some of the official rules around NGO activities in a refugee or IDP context. For example, if you are not injured, shot, or maimed or you have a physical health problem not caused by the conflict, medical treatment cannot be offered:

> *I met an eight-year-old boy with raging eczema. He badly needed medicine but there wasn't any. Imagine that poor boy, in the terrible heat. Another family needed psychiatric drugs, but they couldn't obtain them. Mental health patients become aggressive or even a risk to the people around them. Consequently that family becomes ostracised. It feels as if sadness is piled on top of more sadness.*

Claudia believes it is difficult to remain a kind, generous person in such heartbreaking conditions. She would refuse an offer of tea, which in a Middle Eastern context is part of an important cultural conditioning to give hospitality, because of the appalling hygiene conditions:

> *If these people can't even offer tea anymore, it affects them. They feel terrible. Their energy and positivity drops. People can do a lot to help themselves but not without positivity. People want to be good. They want to be generous. They want dignity. If they lose their self-respect, they become angry people.*

Desires, defences and the role of emotion for the senior leader

Claudia refused to engage in what she termed 'an emotions-based discussion' in relation to her work as a leader in a refugee context. Because she was in Syria when I interviewed her, we were not able to meet face to face, and I was concerned that too high a degree of challenge from me had the potential to provoke a psychologically unmanageable reaction in Claudia. If this happened I would not be able to secure her appropriate help. I wanted to take an ethical approach as well as to protect both of us psychologically.

However, I found different ways of asking her emotion-oriented questions, for example, asking her to 'help me understand what it is like for senior leaders working with refugee crises'. Claudia's specialty is helping people. So, this strategy worked because it satisfied her desire to stay separate from her emotions (or at least, not to reveal them to me), yet it appealed to her ability to observe and report the emotional experiences of others. She was happy to *help me*.

Of course, Claudia's piercing, almost aggressive insistence that we avoid talking about emotions reflects what it can be like to survive as a refugee: It mirrors the shutting down of emotions as a response to trauma, as a way of navigating crisis. Claudia's stance on emotional expression may be important for senior leaders working in crisis-based settings to model to others. Or the opposite could be true.

Sometimes NGO workers are told by their leaders not to go into a refugee camp because of the levels of aggression they may encounter. At best they are verbally attacked because they have turned up, unlike the official agencies (e.g. the local council) who should turn up but do not. Everything that is wrong, is unloaded on to the refugee workers. I can understand why.

As mentioned earlier, Claudia's refusal to discuss emotion was a strong indicator to me, to consider it further. One obvious interpretation is that she has a desire to protect herself psychologically so that she does not absorb the feelings of others and, thus, internalise their trauma. She fears becoming ineffective on the job if her emotions overwhelm her. With insufficient rest and relaxation away from the refugee space, refugee workers at all levels risk becoming co-sufferers or psychologically burnt out.

Claudia's decision to shut out emotion is a defence against pain. It confirms that other person's suffering can cause *us* pain. We risk blaming the very victims of war, rape, famine or natural disasters, for how bad they make us feel. By using denial as a device to tolerate the intolerable nature of other people's suffering, refugee workers find a way of continuing to function. Otherwise they may have to stop doing the very work which so inspires them. They risk shifting from the empowered confident helper poised to rescue to instead a victim who is suffering psychologically or physically or both. This risks rendering them no longer useful, or worse still, a source of damage rather than help.

Outside of the refugee context, leaders may at times choose a similar strategy, in order to keep functioning at work. Some shut down emotionally, or ruthlessly compartmentalise, because of personal circumstances, for example, their wife is being treated for cancer, they are caring for a parent with dementia or, simply, they are finding their job hugely stressful. Shutting down emotionally can be an effective coping strategy for short time. But if used on an ongoing basis it comes at a cost: The cost of emotional connectedness to self and others, both at home and at work. Their relationships and sometimes their own health suffers.

Such leaders may be admired for their calm and their cool, appearing to retain focus and efficiency amidst annoying hiccups or bureaucratic obstacles. However, what is seen on the surface may cover up an inner turmoil which festers. The shutdown leader who has split off from their authentic self is bound to impact the teams they lead and ultimately organisational effectiveness.

In the case of Claudia's work in a refugee context, her conscious decision to evade emotions may serve her well; perhaps it gives her the ability to think slow whilst empathising fast. Such temporary (if indeed they are temporary) defence mechanisms have their place. But it is important for leaders to be aware of when and why they are deploying them. And to take regular rest and relaxation breaks away from the high stress environment. For this reason, aid organisations usually systematise six weekly R&R breaks.

Avoiding overly emotive discussion, or internal engagement with self, may be a worrying sign that a leader's stress levels are unsustainably high or an indication of post-traumatic stress. Claudia desires to repair lives destroyed by war and injustice. She says she can only do this if her emotional defences are secured:

> *I don't think emotional leaders are very helpful. You need people to go in and change something, not just become upset by it.*

I have an interpretation to offer. It concerns Claudia's choice to work in such an intensely emotional, logistical and politically charged environment. These are a set of hypotheses, ideas and notions, but not facts.

Claudia told me she resides in Switzerland, although her everyday working life in recent years has seen her based in the Middle East. She was born in Germany, which during World War II was a crucible of systematic Nazi persecution of Jews, Communists and gay people. The then fascist regime designed and executed a genocide of some 6 million people. Terror and desperation ignited waves of refugees who fled across Europe and Russia, headed for Asia, Australia, Palestine and the Americas – anywhere that would grant them a visa and let them in.

Even though Claudia was born after the end of this period in history, the story of totalitarianism and meticulously curated suffering is an inevitable part of her psychic national inheritance. An inheritance which for many born in post-war Germany generates endless shame, horror and guilt. A discussion in 2017 with Gerard Fromm, a specialist in totalitarianism and the transmission of trauma, highlighted that many Germans have 'devoted themselves to reparation, often directed towards people far away from home'.

We don't know for certain, but consciously or unconsciously Claudia may have a preoccupation with the 'rescue' and assistance of families fleeing across borders and of internally displaced people. The obsessive and seemingly unending need around the world for aid may mirror the unending internal and perhaps unspoken guilt experienced by some Germans. Perhaps giving out aid and compassion creates some form of comfort and rescue or 'aid' for the giver.

In my view, Claudia is repairing the destruction of human beings carried out by her nation in the past. Psychologically, she may be refusing to 'move on', until she has helped 'enough' people. She is refusing to sever her connection or attachment with this past. At the same time, she may outwardly refuse to acknowledge any connection to it. But I can't help thinking that 'she is working in a *camp* after all'.

Claudia no longer lives in the country of her birth, choosing instead the supposed 'neutrality' of Switzerland. A place where she can look out over stunning scenery and heal herself, before going back into the chaos and unsanitary conditions of her work environment.

I may or may not be correct, but the meta-point here is about creativity in our thinking. Developing the ability to use less obvious data to generate possibilities of understanding. These possibilities may offer deeper insights into why people are drawn to do the jobs they do, and why these occupations hold such meaning and motivation. It is important to remember that these are merely ideas, not absolute facts.

Desires and defences – refugees

Having considered some of the desires and defences incurred by a leader in a refugee context, I return to the refugees themselves. In terms of their desires, most refugees simply want to leave the camp. They want to go home. They desire to go back to their old life where they had reached the top of Maslow's[1] pyramid of needs. A life where they read books, had a fulfilling job, had a husband. On a macro level refugees remember that they had a full life, a *home*. Once a refugee, one's preoccupation dips into the micro level of basic survival needs. After shelter and food, people ask for small essentials like a mobile phone charger, nail clippers, chocolate bars or a hair removal kit.

According to Claudia, Arab culture teaches the holding back of emotion in front of guests or outsiders. This may offer a defence of sorts for Syrian or Iraqi refugees to 'hold it together' or contain their despair:

> *As a refugee in a camp, if you start crying you'd wash away – you'd never be able to stop. So, this training, this upbringing, seems to work.*

Maybe this cultural more serves Claudia well too, lest she become compromised by too much emotional expression. Which party – the refugee or the refugee leader – needs this construct most?

Desires and defences – refugee organisations

Let's now consider desire from an organisational perspective. NGOs and aid agencies want to achieve and sustain a good reputation, in order to attract good quality staff and funding. Whether it's a bank, a supermarket chain, a football club or another corporate entity, organisations operating in a refugee context need their work to shine in order to continue to seduce donors. This is particularly the case when crises become longer term, ongoing situations, falling out of the news headlines, even if the humanitarian need is still growing.

There is a contradiction in the desire for money. The back office of an aid agency is expensive to run. Better funded organisations are viewed more favourably yet aid workers say it should be the other way around. Organisations with a humanitarian imperative should want to have spent their money bringing aid to the needy. On one level, they desire to run out of money, not hoard it. But it is seen as a mark of success or status if they have lots of it. Aid workers desire the work they do to run out too. In other words, for the humanitarian crisis to be solved.

In summary, from an organisational perspective, in a refugee context, there is a desire for money and financial status. When it comes to leadership, senior leaders working with refugees want to retain their defences in order to deliver effective change for those they are trying help. They may need to emotionally detach or keep their feelings in a 'regulated state' – somehow connected enough but not overwhelmed by the situation. Managers need to monitor their charges similarly, for them to function well at work and look after their psychological wellbeing. Individual refugees want to return home or set up a new life in another country. Many want to resume where they left off educationally, or in terms of their careers or personal lives. Alongside having some of their desires met, they also want to relinquish some of their defences, knowing that they can live in safety once more.

Eldership, legacy and furnishing future leaders with knowledge

Claudia's career has focused on concern for those in danger. As she nears retirement from hardship postings in the field, Claudia has been reflecting on the survival of her knowledge. She wants to see an officially organised, global system of sharing professional experience. Ideally she believes the state – in her case Switzerland – should capture the richness of learning from senior leaders, to pass on to future leaders and policy makers. Claudia wants to leave a legacy. She wants to build on the concept of eldership.

Claudia's preoccupation with creating a leadership legacy may reflect an anxiety around her own shifting identity and purpose, connected to the prospect of retirement or the death of her working life. Claudia consciously desires to contribute further. And for her contribution to the field of development aid and refugee leadership to sustain. Much of Claudia's career has been spent shepherding people through traumatic endings and into new beginnings. Does she find the approaching ending of her commitment to this a difficult attachment to break?

Working in hostile environments such as conflict zones, refugee camps or places where there is famine or natural disaster often separates people from their family and friends. It is physically and emotionally tough, sometimes even dangerous. To some extent, this is exclusive work. It brings with it a sense of the urgent, the important, the special. Such jobs offer heightened excitement, meaning and drive. With such satisfying and engrossing work, one's identity can become entangled with the job and/or the organisation. It may be worth highlighting how important it is for leaders to consciously develop, retain and defend a life outside of work.

This pertains to those working in other environments where identity can become caught up with the organisation, such as the health service, public service broadcasting, government, social work and teaching. Commercial companies can be equally seductive in terms of self-sacrifice and the development of unhealthy levels of identity and perceived self-worth, which are attached to the job.

The prospect of retirement can pose a different kind of threat, that of exchanging constant occupation with a vacuum. This ending can trigger grieving rather than feeling rewarded for years of dedication in the field. Whilst carrying out important work, there may have been no time, perceived need or energy for anything outside of this. But at the end of a career, is one's contribution remembered? It may not even register as the next crisis hits and another wave of aid workers is deployed.

I believe Claudia desires to make ongoing meaning out of the immense psychological investment she has put into her working life. She needs some part of it to endure once her physical presence in a region or in an organisation has ended. She does not want to fade. Her agreeing to contribute to this book may be part of such a strategy.

At an unconscious emotional level, Claudia may want to retain some sort of umbilical cord – a connection with her work and those she worked for lest *she* become the 'refugee' – the one without a 'home', i.e. an identity: One who has crossed a border [into retirement] and cannot return.

Claudia's desire to make a lasting difference, or even form part of a national legacy, offers potential for increased organisational or societal efficiency. It may also be a version of nation building through developing a professional leadership collective, which as we know is her management ethos on a micro level with her team. But a collective leadership knowledge bank could hinder new ideas emerging from a new generation of leaders.

In the next part of this chapter we hear from a young volunteer worker, moved by news reports of refugees making their way to Europe from war-torn Syria and from Afghanistan. Aged 19, Holly negotiated a year out from her university degree to help in two refugee centres: Calais in Northern France and Thessaloniki in Greece.

The young volunteer refugee camp worker

> *The leadership in Calais, in Northern France, was shocking. Nobody knew what they were doing. People came with absolutely no training or experience. Most were under 27 years old. The vast majority thought they'd go and help for two weeks. When they realised nobody else was taking a leadership role and that what they were offering was better than nothing, people stayed months turning into gap years and even leaving university altogether.*

Holly's job was in the distribution warehouse. Every day she and her colleagues arrived at the Camp in Calais ready to give out bedding, pillows, saucepans, toothbrushes and razors. She opened up the back of the van, to face a sea of muddy paths, tents and shanty style shelters. There were 10,000 people in need. People from Syria, Afghanistan, Libya, Algeria, Iran and Iraq. Holly found herself saying 'no' and apologising to people whom she knew were desperate. All she had to offer were randomly donated items, and she did not have enough of them.

When the Calais camp, known colloquially as 'The Jungle', was shut down in 2016 by the French authorities, hoping to disperse or disappear the problem of refugees and economic migrants, Holly moved to Greece. There she helped in another refugee camp. Again she had to refuse people vital items of clothing and cooking equipment. Beneath what might appear cruel or even callous behaviour was an attempt to be fair.

The camp set up a donated clothing boutique based on a points system. It was a way of ensuring that nobody had absolutely nothing. Each person was given 150 points, which were renewed each month. A T-shirt was worth 20 points, trousers cost 50 points.

But in response to the points system, a black market sprang up. People clubbed their points together and bought ten T-shirts, then sold sell them within the Camp. In both France and Greece, Holly observed mafia-style activities going on within the refugee camps, not just with clothes but with drugs, weapons and accommodation. For example, in Calais, there were a limited number of caravans. These were intended as more solid shelters for families. But organised gangs of single men forced or paid families to move out of them. This reflects the nature of the environment. In a tropical rainforest or 'jungle', there is a rich abundance of food and resources for those with the survival skills to navigate this hostile domain.

In such a context, psychological desires and defences abound, both for refugees and for aid workers. Holly described the refugee camps where she worked as bleak, clinical and segregated places, full of despair, trauma and need:

> *Every refugee is in a camp because they want something better. They are driven by the desire to find shelter, protection and respite from war.*

But the refugee camps do not necessarily offer psychological or physical safety:

> *These camps can be highly individualistic places. People are here because nobody else has been able to protect or look after them. There's a huge aspect of self-defence.*

This can translate as physical or psychological 'attack' on another person or group, as people squabble over limited resources to survive. Refugee or migrant camps can be dangerous places, rather than places associated with refuge or safety.

The desire for sex in a predominantly male refugee environment such as in Calais, France, may not have been explicitly articulated by refugee workers nor policy makers, but it would have been there. As would the desire by both men and women for protection from violence or violation.

In both France and Greece, volunteer workers shared a desire to help, yet had to remain, at times, highly defended:

> *I would feel physically and mentally tired. At times I felt desperate and a bit hopeless. A few bad days with things not running smoothly could be very depressing. Without the volunteer community it would have been impossible for me to keep going.*

Holly's emotional 'shelter' came from the other people volunteering, in addition to the fuel of kindnesses they experienced from the refugees themselves. Both helped maintain psychological strength, reinforcing the desire to continue the work.

As with Claudia, Holly, also wishes that refugee camps did not need to exist. Both women observed the suffering of traumatised adults and children. The absence of school. The interruption of university or a flourishing career. The chaos of extended families who had become separated across multiple borders. Sometimes they observed the collapse of hope.

As a way of breaking the relentless work required of women, the camp in Greece instigated a 'Women's Hour'. This weekly gathering reflected a desire to give some form of comfort, containment and relief from the emotional distress of daily life for refugee women. It acknowledged their need for psychological support in a context which lacked the expertise or resources for it. However, the 'Women's Hour' created a space, for one hour, once a week where women could congregate for tea, some biscuits and a chance to pamper themselves a little with some donated beauty products. It was not enough, but it was something. It was greatly appreciated and helped make life a little less bleak. It was a slither of time where women could leave their suffering and literally embrace each other with hugs and smiles. It offered a chance to let down their defences – their need to cope.

Reflecting on what makes for effective leadership in a refugee context, from the perspective of a young volunteer worker like Holly, the importance of ego-free management emerges:

> *Defensive leaders who are offended if people disagree with them become overly attached to their idea rather than able to evaluate it. They miss better solutions because their own injury is caught up in their leadership decisions.*

In Holly's case, many of her leaders were untrained and inexperienced. Some became traumatised by the very environment they were hoping to improve. This is understandable. But it is an indulgence that already stretched aid agencies – both formal and informal – have little or no resources to address. Better to be mindful and proactive suggests Holly:

> *Leaders who've over-invested and been working too hard, without appropriate support or self-awareness, start to become needy of recognition. Because they've lost quite a lot of themselves to being in a refugee context, they can't accept*

> *failure nor the idea that they may have made a mistake. For example, providing psychological support for the unimaginable traumatic events people had been through. In my view well-intentioned but inexperienced leaders probably caused more damage. They also ended up with secondhand trauma themselves.*

Whilst the untrained, emergent leader risks being insufficiently professional, their unpaid colleagues may go the other way. They may not think of their volunteering as a 'proper job', when it is. Compared to the well-meaning but disorganised, emergent leadership structure in the Calais refugee camp, the set-up in Greece was more professional. For Holly, this offered a better example of what leadership in a refugee context should look like:

> *My coordinator in Greece was a qualified social worker with leadership training. She spoke Arabic. She connected with the refugees. She listened and communicated with us well too. This leader was open to other people's thinking and suggestions. She tried things but was prepared to change the plan if it didn't work.*

Formal rules, management structures including a hierarchy and appropriate emotional boundaries created healthier role models of best practice and emotional self-management.

Desires and defences: the young volunteer worker

Volunteers want to help. They desire to learn and embrace life experiences which may form their future careers or political stances. Naturally Holly desired personal safety. She also desired a defence against the pain of refusing aid to the needy, because there was not enough to go around. Her psychological defences or justifications included trying to be fair.

From a leadership perspective, the many young volunteers working for small grassroots refugee organisations enjoy the lack of hierarchy associated with established, cumbersome and bureaucratic larger organisations. Some prefer a flat leadership structure, where everyone's opinion feels valued. Whilst lack of hierarchy can be refreshing and dexterous, it can at times compromise the clarity of who is in charge. More interesting is that the shape of such organisations is partly a response to – or a defence against – the strongly hierarchical structures of government, which some young volunteers blame for contributing to the causes of recent refugee crises.

Structures aside, workers at the start of their careers need ego-free leadership from well-trained, well-boundaried, appropriately skilled leaders. They also need sleep and time out, as a defence against burn out or assimilated trauma. Note the juxtaposition of university undergraduates interrupting or even desiring to leave their studies to assist in a refugee camp. Versus the refugees they are trying to help, many of whom were forced to leave and lose *their* educational opportunity.

Holly represents the classic position of youth: Idealism, energy and critique. She finds aspects of government and global policy function depressing. Her interpretation is that there is an apathy or a failure by those with power to use their influence to change things. Or at least to try. Holly also challenges leaders to honestly appraise whether they are the right person to do their job. To consider the effect of a leadership position on themselves as an individual and on those who lead.

A host community in a refugee context

Next, we hear what it is like from the perspective of a 'host community' which experiences a sudden influx of refugees. Noori grew up in Peshawar in Pakistan, at a time when 2.5 million Afghan refugees crossed the border into her country. What people assumed would be temporary refugee camps were still there 25 years later.

> *We were already a poor country. So, the impact of 2.5 million Afghans pouring over our border was enormous. Our infrastructure collapsed. There wasn't enough water or electricity for everyone. Rents rose beyond what local people could afford to pay. Our home culture teaches us hospitality and kindness towards outsiders. But not integration.*

Unusually, Noori was brought up in a mixed marriage in Pakistan. Growing up around Afghan refugees was consistent with her family's diverse thinking and acceptance of outsiders. Pakistani culture perceives itself as sharing much in common with neighbouring Afghanistan, from clothes to religious and social customs to certain facial features. But as the Afghans' Mercedes buses crossed the border into Pakistan, a foreboding sense of invasion and otherness emerged in the psyche of the host community.

Rents rose sharply as multiple Afghan families squeezed into apartments designed for just one family. Collectively Afghans could afford to pay more and local landlords were happy to take the money. Some Pakistani families found themselves homeless. Because of the housing shortage, slums developed in parks and public spaces. Girls felt unsafe as places previously of sanctuary and enjoyment became rowdy and overcrowded. Robbery and assault increased, or was perceived to increase. As with the Syrian and Iraqi refugee context, the issue of distinguishing genuine asylum seekers from terrorists surfaced in host communities in Pakistan.

With an extra 2.5 million people drawing on the water and electricity supplies, the already strained infrastructure in some cities, like Peshawar, collapsed. There was no billing system. The roads were clogged with Afghan lorries and impromptu Afghan bus companies.

An interesting conflict presented itself. This time, instead of attending to the Afghan refugees' fears that their hierarchy of needs may not be met (Maslow's hierarchy of needs mentioned earlier in this chapter), the concern was that the host community may be suffering an almost identical angst. It may be losing its most basic needs, as the newcomers ensure their needs are also met. This seemingly more vulnerable group may appear to take over the host community rather than merge into it. One can sense the competitive threat.

The desire in the host population shifts from welcoming the war torn and needy to a drive for self-protection; local people fear their jobs and businesses will be usurped by the refugee influx. Even the most basic needs such as shelter and water may no longer be able to be met because of the inability of the system to cope with so many new arrivals. Such turning inwards of concern – something evident in much wealthier economies such as Germany, France and the UK, in relation to actual or feared waves of immigration – was difficult to reconcile for Noori's community because of its culturally ingrained obligation or honour, of protecting someone who is running for their life.

Noori's grandmother made food for refugee families in the neighbouring apartments. On another occasion she took a meal to a flat inhabited by a group of bachelors. Through the open door she saw Kalashnikov rifles piled up to the ceiling. These were fighters not refugees, explains Noori.

> *Imagine having all that ammunition stored in a residential area. These fighters were friendly and used to play with us children, but they were dangerous men.*

Thus, we see the complexity of cultural, economic and social issues evoked for communities faced with a surge of refugees or migrants.

Less of a physical danger, but psychologically perturbing, was the impact on the local population of Afghan traders who set up gold, transport and other businesses. Afghans were hired over Pakistani labourers because they were perceived to be stronger and cheaper. This is a reversal of the situation following the fall of the Taliban regime in Afghanistan and the election in 2004 of President Hamid Karzai. Then, Afghanistan ceded major construction and infrastructure projects to Pakistani workers who were seen as more skilled and entrepreneurial. Unlike Afghans, Pakistanis' education hadn't been interrupted by three decades of war followed by six years of drought.

When I first worked in Afghanistan in 2005, I saw young unemployed Afghan men congregated by the roadside, disillusioned, depressed, unskilled [or rather, de-skilled through schools being regularly closed when they were children]. They were unable to provide for their families. At the time, even Afghans joked about how whatever they made broke. Better to hire a Pakistani.

Desires and defences for the host community

The first desire from the refugee host community's perspective was the desire to help. Also a desire to obey their cultural concept of honour, which includes welcoming the outsider or the visitor. But it would appear that many Afghans arrived with confidence, finance and solid business plans. In contrast to many refugee communities, Afghans appeared empowered. Instead of being the vulnerable newcomers, they rendered – at least from some local people's perspectives – the host community vulnerable to a version of 'refugee' status of its own: A fear of losing their jobs or the ability to afford to continue living in their home city. Those one assumed were vulnerable or even destitute turned out to be potent creators of insecurity and even homelessness in others.

For the host community both desires and psychological defences were fully engaged. The word *jihad* means 'struggle'. This refers to both external struggle but also to an internal struggle: That of being a good person. Host communities such as Noori's tried to reconcile their attachment to their philosophy with the practicalities of coping with the multiple impacts of the new immigrants.

The host community held a desire to address the root causes of this mass immigration. Both because it was causing suffering to Afghans but also because it threatened their own limited resources. Surprisingly there was little intermarriage or integration between the two populations.

Generally, there was a cultural desire to welcome refugees but to retain a separation. A defence against assimilation and loss of family identity. A desire to remain boundaried however overcrowded and intermingled living conditions became. Unsurprisingly, as happens in many in-group, out-group contexts, there is a pattern of demonising the outsiders as unclean, less refined and the cause of increased crime.

In the case of Pakistani host communities, hostility and the engagement of psychological defences increased over time. As domestic terrorism grew, rifts between the refugee and host population also grew. Conflict often lessens through contact. But in this case, proximity produced a culture of blame.

For more open-minded individuals such as Noori, the levels of hostility and scapegoat behaviours in the host community were shocking. I interpret these raw, primitive human responses to be part of the way we access our own 'internal refugee'. That of connecting with feelings of emotional disorientation or logistical displacement. This could be linked to previous trauma, inherited experience or to early attachment bonds formed as children.

Closing thoughts

Through exploring the perspectives of Claudia, a senior leader and Holly the young volunteer worker, we see the imperative of having well-trained, psychologically contained, experienced and ego-free leaders in a refugee context. It is also important for leaders to appropriately self-regulate or at least monitor their emotions, in order to remain psychologically healthy and effective at work.

Leaders in such environments must be sufficiently rivetted[2] yet detached from the task, lest the emotional aspects and secondhand trauma compromise their ability to function. The same applies to those they lead. In addition to being affected or even incapacitated by the trauma of others is the risk of blaming the disadvantaged for how bad they may make those who are trying to help them feel.

This is an example of projective identification. Most of us project our feelings onto others, often without realising it, sometimes in quite ordinary situations which frustrate us. In extreme circumstances, this temporary defence mechanism, can damage the do-er and risks damaging those they aim to help. As we know, these people may already be suffering beyond what is reasonable to bear.

Leaders need to recognise behavioural and emotional triggers in themselves and in their teams, which indicate that psychological support is needed. Even better, to take preventative action at an early stage.

Burn out, the prospect of retirement or moving on to the next crisis risks creating a pattern of lost learning. This leaves the next set of leaders poorly defended against repeating the same mistakes, reducing or slowing success. A conscious endeavour to value eldership would see the systematic capturing and sharing of knowledge and learning about what creates effective leadership in a refugee or other humanitarian context.

This chapter has considered that not all 'refugees' are truly seeking refuge from war and suffering. Some are economic migrants in search of a better life. The refugee context creates opportunities for corruption, exploitation and dominance. There are business deals to be cut. Organised gangs use waves of migration as a blanket under which to run lucrative people-smuggling operations. They profiteer from vulnerability and desperation.

In addition, there seems to be no coherent public policy on how to handle people simply seeking a better life. Nor a mechanism to successfully separate 'good' refugees from 'bad' people on the move.

Although not expanded upon in this chapter, it is worth reflecting on the longer-term effects of refugee or IDP status and which desires or defences continue to influence thinking and behavioural responses, long after the immediate crisis has subsided. Some reactive behaviours may only surface once the need for temporary shelter or resettling appears to have been resolved. In other words, once the immediate emergency is 'over'.

Added to this is the potential societal impact of secondhand trauma or transmitted trauma from today's refugee generation to future, as yet unborn generations with refugee ancestry. This notion of transgenerationally transmitted trauma can be defined as:

> *When the members of an affected group* [in this case refugees], *cannot reverse their shame, humiliation, helplessness and dehumanisation and cannot mourn their losses, they obligate the subsequent generation(s) through what is known as the transgenerational transmission of trauma to complete these unfinished psychological processes.*
>
> (Volkan and Fowler 2009, p. 217)

Transgenerational transmission of trauma, ongoing annihilation anxiety or repetitive nightmares are not explored in further depth in this chapter. But I highlight its importance as a concept, because of the potential for long-term psychological fallout of decisions made by policy makers and government leaders today; an unintended or naïve legacy, which tomorrow's leaders will have to address.

Such consequences may ripple out across society, and demand further financial and psychological resources, potentially decades after the visible crisis has subsided. Leaders in industry and the public sector may find themselves the employers of traumatised refugees or descendants of refugees who carry an inherited family experience. Both experiences are likely to inform attitudes, behaviours, leadership styles and diversity of contribution to the workplace.

Another aspect of many refugee crises is the perspective of the host community. Noori described some of the desires and defences in play, including a fear that there may not be 'enough'. For example, stretched physical resources such as infrastructure, housing and jobs. Such complex and conflicting emotions are uncomfortable and, even if accompanied by compassion and a will to help, understandable.

Organisational consultant and former refugee Itamar Rogovsky argues that in a way we are all 'refugees' (Rogovsky 2017). We are all human beings in search of comfort and safety. From the moment we leave the womb – a warm, cosy, containing, familiar space – we are forced into the bright, cold and strange environment of the outside world. Birth is a metaphor for the refugee experience: being forced to leave the comfort of one's country of origin, to cope with a daunting, uncertain, potentially unsafe new environment where survival is not guaranteed. Eventually it is likely that new, comforting associations and alternative sources of nourishment will establish themselves. These will sit on a bedrock of what went before, in terms of previous culture and the endured traumas of the experience of exit.

Rogovsky emphasises that we should not distance ourselves from refugee crises. For they are more relevant to us than perhaps we realise:

> *Anyone who dislikes refugees dislikes themselves. If they cannot tolerate refugees, they are saying that they cannot tolerate a part of themselves.*

From this statement, we can see the value of first investigating ourselves before forming opinions or conceiving policy approaches.

Desires and defences: leadership in a refugee context

Reflections for leaders

- What is your connection to the concept of 'refugee'?
- When are you or have you been a 'refugee' – literally or metaphorically?
- When have you felt like an 'internally displaced person'?
- When has your department or your organisation felt 'displaced'?
- In your role, what are your desires?
- What defences do you have or want?
- What desires and defences do you observe in those you work with?
- What organisational desires and defences are in play?
- When have you witnessed an equivalent to 'The Jungle' at work? What have been the consequences?
- What psychological 'inheritance' may influence you in your choice of work? Or the way you work?

Reflections for coaches

- Maslow's hierarchy of needs – what are the needs in your office?
- Who are the 'bee keepers' (guardians of safety or the guardians of others) in your working context?
- When might you have taken the role of 'bee keeper' at work?
- When were you the vulnerable new arrival in a work or home context?
- When might your arrival have posed a threat to the 'host' community in the office?
- How did you feel if you were the cause of someone else's suffering e.g. making them redundant or refusing to promote them – creating a refugee or ejected person in the workplace?

Notes

1 Maslow's model of human need included in this order, the need for: food, water, warmth and rest (for which read also shelter). After this comes security, safety, intimate relationships and, later, the need to self-actualise. In other words, if you have the potential to become an engineer or a teacher, you are likely to do this but only once more basic physiological and emotional needs are met first.

2 The concept of listening with 'rivetted detachment' is a term coined by Liz Macann, former head of coaching at the BBC.

References

Maslow, A. H. (1943). A theory of human motivation. *Psychological Review*, 50(4), 370–396.

Dr Itamar Rogovsky. Informal Conversation at ISPSO Annual General Meeting, Copenhagen, 2017.

United Nations Refugee Agency, UNHCR. Definition of a Refugee. www.unrefugees.org/refugee-facts/what-is-a-refugee/

Volkan, V. and Fowler C. (2009). Large group narcissism and political leadership. *Psychiatric Annals*, 39(4), 217.

Suggested reading

Fromm, M. G. (2012). *Lost in Transmission: Studies of Trauma Across Generations*. London: Karnac.

Chapter 9

Communism cripples character

The story of how transition from political oppression to free democracy unleashed waves of innovation, capitalism, lies and laziness

I'm speechless. I feel guilty. Guilty for telling you all this. Reading my story – these thoughts and feelings – I have tears in my eyes. It's strong. It's full. It's sad, yet beautiful. The insights which accompany my story would never have crossed my mind. I know now that I didn't want the inner voice to speak out. It's almost a shock for me. What an inside look. Thanks for sharing a part of my life with me.

This is the story of a national divorce. A wave of upheaval and change, as seen through the eyes of a Czech teenager. The idea for this case study emerged at my local hairdresser's. The receptionist approached me to apologise for a mix-up over my appointment. The resulting conversation, prompted by my appreciation of the receptionist's honesty and professionalism, was one about quality of character, individual ethical choice points, systemic corruption and enforced perspectives. It encompassed authority, power and societal change. This case study is an individual's story about how people adapt, comply, fight back and innovate under oppression. Its analysis of experiences such as betrayal and hopelessness, hypocrisy and protection offers leaders a provocation to think about centres of control, whether they adhere to their stated values and where there are conflicts between the personal and the organisational ideology.

As a coach, one is constantly interested in other people's history and experience, helping leaders explore rich seams of insight and integrate their learning from multiple different sources. The subject for this case study – a former railways and logistics manager, now international relations student and mother – is not a current or former coaching client. The nature our relationship was one of two professional women, energised by each other's different perspectives. Through exploring Renata's story, we developed interpretive meaning together.

Renata – who did not want her name changed – found the guilt evoked by sharing her story surprising. It may be a symptom of legacy. If one were to analyse the nature of our conversation from a coaching perspective, it would be one of enquiry, deeper probing and invitation to analyse the impact of authoritarian leadership from a personal and national narrative.

I use Renata's testimony, reporting what she saw and what she felt, to illustrate aspects of coercive control, notions of equality, failure of empathy, thriving corruption and unintended legacy. Her narrative shows how entrepreneurialism and innovation can blossom under oppression. It is fascinating to hear about the various motivations and behaviours which resulted, including how their legacy threads through people's thinking long afterwards.

Communism cripples character: the story of how transition from political oppression to free democracy unleashed waves of innovation, capitalism, lies and laziness

Communism crippled our people's character . . .

Ecstasy and the embracing of change

Renata was 17 years old when her country of birth, then called Czechoslovakia, split into two countries: The Czech Republic and Slovakia. It was 1993. The process of separation took 4 years, but it began with a 12-day revolution: A Velvet Revolution. A national divorce and non-violent transition of power, from Communist oppression to free democracy. It was a huge social and systemic change which touched both personal and family lives, as well as organisational structures and how people did business.

Almost overnight, jeans, Mickey Mouse T-shirts and Haribo sweets were embraced as exciting representations of the Imperialist freedoms enjoyed in Europe and America. People felt desperate to travel. Language schools and travel agencies sprang up, eager to capitalise [sic] on and sate the hunger of a people starved of contact with the outside world.

Decades of institutionalised hatred of the capitalist West appeared to dissolve, to be replaced by a celebration of freedom, new hope and opportunity. This was accompanied by individual self-empowerment and the taking up of authority over self, i.e. inhabiting the 'adult' position rather than being stuck in 'child' mode. People were suddenly free to go on holiday, learn a language, start a business and openly express their political views. The relationship with authority and power began to change internally (psychologically), as well as externally.

Renata remembers the ecstatic excitement; the feelings of yearning and disbelief. The Berlin Wall came down. Swiftly followed by the Iron Curtain that was the Soviet Bloc. It was like a wave, as democracy came to one East European country after another. The notion of a wave evokes a similar sense of opportunity and desired hope evident in the Arab Spring, a movement which started in 2011 and called for peaceful social change across the Arab World. Back in Czechoslovakia, Renata and her family watched events unfold on Austrian TV news:

> *There were protests and singing. People shouted: 'Please go!' The authorities packed up and left. It was like a civil war, without blood. Bringing down a government is nearly always paid for in human lives. What I'm so proud of is how this huge change happened without violence.*

Renata's family was ecstatic. The immediate reaction of her parents was to travel. The family drove to Vienna to see the Christmas tree. It was just 100 km down the road. Some people had waited 50 years to be able to get in their car and go, without asking permission from their boss or the local council. Or without having to leave their children behind, as collateral against defection.

This newfound freedom was both physical and psychological. People didn't know how to handle freedom and democracy. There was a frenzied reaction to the experience of change. There was the panic of transition. Renata analyses the human behaviours which resulted:

> *It was like animals being released from a cage. People were frenziedly doing business; there was selfishness, corruption, sharing and refusal to share. . . it was a sea of survival behaviours.*

Properties and businesses which had been confiscated by the state's Communist government in 1948 were given back. But there was chaos. There was no legal framework to repatriate what belonged to whom. There was no systemic coping mechanism to enable this to happen successfully. People assumed their country would go back to its former wealth and success. But it didn't. Instead people sold their businesses to foreign investors. They extracted their money while they could, afraid that their assets could be seized again at any time. Says Renata:

> *So, in a way, nothing belonged to us, again.*

Renata was thrilled with the new President Vaclav Havel. She regarded him as a wonderful human being. Vaclav Havel may have been out of his depth in terms of leading a nation, yet he was heading up the change so many people thirsted for:

> *He was a wonderful leader. He didn't even ask to be President. It was the we, the people who asked him to lead us. And he did so in such an honest and humble way. But for all his humanity, he didn't know how to run an economy.*

Partly as a result, this critical period of transition turned out to be a great opportunity to buy, sell, profiteer and corrupt:

> *It was like a jungle. I think mistakes were understandable and to be expected.*

The release from Communism – a political and social ideology, which was supposed to be about equality, contribution and community ownership – certainly produced some dramatic responses. Whilst the regime was still in power, there was plenty of corruption and entrepreneurialism – quite some distance from the concept of fairness for all.

Amongst Renata's family and friends Communism became a bit of a joke. People scoffed at it. They viewed Communism as fake. A big hypocrisy. People knew the outside world was not about Porsches and luxury and homelessness. They knew it was about brainwashing. Ordinary citizens were told that people in Europe and America were rich, and that there was homelessness everywhere and that this was caused by competition. They were told people could lose their jobs. That you have to pay for education and healthcare. That this so-called Imperialistic lifestyle caused divorce and family breakdown.

Secrecy and the myth of equality

The principle of Communism was that everyone was equal. So those who were average, lazy or unqualified flew up the career ladder. Lucrative jobs were typically allocated to best friends or family members. A good doctor or teacher was paid the same salary as a bad one. Says Renata:

> *People were asking 'what's the point of trying hard because we still have the same job and the same salary, as the person who doesn't do his or her job well, and leaves after lunch?'*

Renata believes Communism's supposed equality ruined morale and infected individuals' character. She says it halted people's personal growth and limited their potential. And here's the hypocrisy: whilst ordinary people queued around the block for winter shoes, their Communist leaders bought properties abroad and enjoyed luxury holidays. On every level, many people tried to better their prospects, by finding ways to work the System:

> *The butcher would hide the best meat to bribe officials. He wanted to make sure his daughter graduated. Or that the best surgeon operated on his wife. There was so little in the shops to buy, that people stole. They would sell and profiteer. Anyone with access to power would abuse their power.*

Renata reveals that many older people complain about the competitive lifestyle of Capitalism. Some even wish for the return of the idealised 'good old days'. It would seem that life outside the womb – an enclosed, restricted, familiar space – can be a difficult adaptation to make after spending 40 years of your life in a secure place. There are risks to freedom and independence of thought when people have become used to being deprived of it. Being 'stuck' has its comforts, whereas change can feel unsafe or destabilising. We see parallel patterns in organisations where senior leaders, employees or sometimes union representatives who, having become invested in a status of 'stuck', are resistant to leaving their entrenched position however much they may claim to campaign for change. Perversely there may be unacknowledged 'rewards' which maintain stasis and corporate suffering.

Instead of equality and community, life behind the Iron Curtain seemed to stimulate at once apparent compliance and raging entrepreneurialism. There was both internal and external rebellion. The concept of sharing combined with one of selfish endeavour. Under Communism people were forced to seek permission from the authorities for everything. For example, a permit had to be obtained to go on holiday. The authorities would ask neighbours about each other, whether someone was a good Communist, whether a person's wife was faithful. Perhaps the authorities' questions about adultery represented the leadership's fear of unfaithfulness and desertion by ordinary people whom they sought to control. The resulting human response was to tell lies. People sent anonymous letters, informing on each other. Marriage, abortion, divorce – these private matters were all publicly discussed by the authorities. People pretended everything was perfect, in case anyone spoke out.

It is hardly surprising that couples kept secret plans. Some feared creating problems for their friends. Others did not. Citizens issued anonymous slights against each other. They became constantly suspicious. Someone might claim that a family wanted to emigrate. The authorities would confiscate their passports for years. Even in today's Czech Republic, Renata observes that when things are not going perfectly for someone, those around them almost seem to enjoy it. Such collective envy appears at times to perpetuate in the national psyche as part of the legacy of Communism.

Renata remembers the day that a family in her parents' apartment block disappeared. They had defected. Overnight. Without telling anyone. A letter arrived months later, explaining and apologising for not telling them:

> *There were tear stains on the letter. It was clear to us that the person writing it was crying,'* recalls Renata. *They knew that they had to protect us, and in the letter, they said 'you never did anything . . . you had no idea of our intention. You didn't cooperate . . .' We waited ten years before we could see these friends again.*

So, whilst the environment produced considerable psychological aggression, it also contained degrees of compassion, empathy and care to protect people other than the self.

In the 1970s and 1980s, Renata's parents were given permission to visit some friends in Germany, but only on the condition that they left their two children behind. Permission to leave came with an obligation to come back. After their holiday, the couple was required to report in at a hearing. The authorities wanted to know if they had spoken to any Westerners.

The same German friends would send parcels of sweets and children's clothes for Renata and her brother. Every package arrived opened and tampered with. The sweets were half eaten. Four out of five dresses had been stolen.

The ongoing impact of authoritarian rule continues to be visible today. Czech citizens dislike like being given directives from the EU, for example, on issues such as whether to accept Syrian or Afghan immigrants. It evokes the old regime's style of receiving commands from a headquarters elsewhere. Then it was Moscow, Russia. Now it is Brussels, Belgium. For many people who lived under Communist rule, the EU symbolises a larger control centre. It is a symbol of the exhaustion of Communism.

Renata's parents' recent decision to buy her brother an apartment offers another insight into how systemic programming can seep into the subconscious thinking and consequent decision making of even those opposed to a regime. Renata explains:

> *My parents think I have a luxurious lifestyle because I live in the West, so they bought my brother a flat in the Czech Republic. He has no job. He sleeps on the sofa all day. Then my parents realised how unfair they had been and decided to leave me their apartment in their wills. My mother asked me: 'Are you happy now?' I said: 'No. How can I be happy when having a flat comes at a price of you not being there?'*

So, Renata's brother has no job and a flat, whilst Renata, a single parent coming out of a violent marriage to an Englishman, lives in rented accommodation in London. Her parents – who prayed for an end to Communism – appear to have absorbed some of its egalitarian ideals. They are subconsciously trying to make both siblings 'equal', by giving the 'less fortunate' one a flat. Whilst their 'more fortunate' daughter must wait decades for a similar gift. Waiting decades, being another element of living under Communist rule.

Renata's brother's behaviour may be independent from his experiences as a child under Communism. But if this is not the case, his passive and depressive lifestyle (as opposed an alternative response of active, restless, anger) seems to represent a resignation to powerlessness and lack of control – a hopelessness. It would be an assumption to think that such hopelessness or depression dissipates once freedom arrives. Change at this point – however much desired it may be – can prove too frightening to embrace. The impact of oppression cannot be rinsed away.

Hopelessness is another understandable response to authoritarianism. Individual behaviours may again represent another part of a national legacy. The two contrasting siblings offer us in turn, the proactive get up and go (literally) as a reaction to freedom. Compare this to the continued attachment to a passive apathy of acceptance and inaction, holding on to the victim stance of living under oppression. These two character traits demonstrate an external representation of splitting (Klein 1960). Under healthy conditions people feel both happiness and sadness. They can 'hold' both, rather like being sporty and active, then laid back and restful. A healthy way of being is to integrate the two stances. The two siblings represent an inability to integrate.

These contrasting positions resonate with the behaviour sometimes observed in enormous, long established, stable, blue-chip organisations which refuse to or cannot respond to changing circumstances with spontaneity and zest. Its staff sometimes embodies similar qualities. Compare this to a start-up culture where nimble dexterity is part of a new company's high, positive, emergent and iterative corporate energy. These descriptions may be a bit of a cliché, but ideally organisations and their staff would do well to adopt – or integrate – aspects of both sets of attributes.

There are bound to be many more examples of individual and societal legacy following the collapse of Communism, from an appreciation of freedom to the long-term impact – even trauma – of many years lived in pretence, distrust, watchfulness and fear. This applies to those forced to live under Communism but also for those who imposed, complied and colluded with it.

A look beneath the surface

Renata's childhood and teenage years, under Communism, offer multiple opportunities to dip beneath the surface. People reacted to the mass nationalisation of assets. Then to persecution and oppression. They reacted internally, inter-personally and systemically. This community, which was answerable to Russia, fractured into two nations, which were suddenly expected to run themselves. During Communism, individualistic, competitive, self-orientated, oppressive survival behaviours intermingled with a veneer of equality and conformity. Coincidentally, identical entrepreneurial and corrupt behaviours erupted, both as a response to freedom and as a strategy to cope with domination. These responses are part of a natural repertoire of human behaviours. But they become exaggerated, or employed differently, during and after extreme experiences.

Freudian theory points to the division of the mind into the punishing 'super-ego', the processed 'ego' and the childlike 'id'. The regime supplied the 'super-ego' (Freud 1940). This way, individuals did not have to develop their own moral compass. People did not need to make decisions about right and wrong. Instead, the authorities assumed the role of critical parent. As a result, people did not take responsibility for their actions. Passive aggressive blame developed. People became adept at holding a duality of pretence and distrust and apparent obedience of the rules.

The leadership lessons from Renata's story offer us space to think about the price society and individuals pay, because of a national [or organisational] state of mind. At work, leaders may appear happy and capable. Yet beneath the surface they may lack confidence, experience or the knowledge that change is afoot. Their duality may be about holding confidentiality about certain organisational goings on, whilst at the same time playing the role of a trustworthy leader.

Renata's experience of an abusive marriage in the UK perhaps demonstrates again the living of a double life. Apparently happy, settled and 'successful' on the outside, Renata endured physical and emotional threat within the confines of her home. Her attraction to her then husband mirrors an attraction to the familiar in terms of the butcher, the teacher, the surgeon. These people were not at all like her own emotionally expressive father. But rather, they represent certain elements within a society where she had had to learn to survive. This illustrates the concept of how individuals can be attracted to or adaptive to systemic or organisational constructs.

Alan Bookbinder, a student of Russian and former BBC documentary maker during the Cold War, regularly stepped behind the Iron Curtain, returning to Western Europe with rich political and social insights:

> *Just like Renata's parents, people learned to live two different lives. Many paid lip service to the system, echoing anti-Western propaganda in public, never revealing their true thoughts, except at home, in the presence of trusted close family or friends. They remained suspicious of others, even hostile, to people they didn't know well.*

But in private, it was the opposite. Away from the gaze of the regime's informers, who were everywhere, people joked about the System. They dreamed of freedom and democracy. They coveted books, art and freedom of expression.

Political commentator and pro-European Richard Laming comments on the impact of authoritarian regimes and external, controlling systems, such as that described by Renata:

> *One of the best criticisms of a totalitarian system is that it distorts incentives. That includes not only economic behaviour but also social behaviour, which is worse. It is no accident that revolutionary movements challenge social and family life. Some leaders work within organisations that have myths and shibboleths*[1]*that must be observed and respected, even in the knowledge that they are false. Learning how to follow those rules and when to break them is something everyone needs helps with. I include myself in that.*

The ability of leaders to discern whether and when they are working in some sort of repressive arrangement is important. A bullying culture at work may not appear to be the same as a national totalitarian regime, but it has echoes of a society that everyone knows exists and learns to adapt to or work with. Or that no one dares leave. Similarly with individual's beliefs and values, which do not always align with their organisation's stance.

Leaders and employees need to decide whether they can reconcile any disconnect, working out how to conform in public without losing a sense of self in private. The building of trust and rapport without being hypocritical or totally selfish is a challenge. Some elements of coming to work cannot be reconciled perfectly. But crucially, leaders must challenge orthodoxy in their place of work, in such a way that they are not ostracised or do not ostracise others who challenge the status quo. Above all, we must all work out how to maintain self-respect and authenticity in all this.

Closing thoughts

Renata's story shows us examples of how people respond to massive change. We see their reactions to oppression, hypocrisy and injustice. Her observations exemplify on a national scale what it can feel like when effort is not rewarded, nor laziness or lack of dedication questioned. The model of non-competitiveness to create an equal society offers employers operating in free market economies some important insights. Appraisals, promotion, pay raises, bonuses and other forms of recognition, including implicit, not just explicit, rewards, need to be 'done right'.

Employees need their leaders to set genuine goals. Senior managers must be seen to act upon their own 360-degree feedback, before expecting junior staff to do likewise. It can be hard for senior leaders who are already pretty busy with their day jobs to make the effort and find the energy to switch off a suite of unconscious habits they may have been repeating for years.

However, their organisation needs them to try. This is their deeper work. It is analogous to fighting against, versus continuing to display behaviours from, the old regime. Many of us may harbour an 'old regime' within ourselves. Sometimes one of our making, sometimes not. This inner 'harbour' may shelter us from certain difficulties, or even enable us to avoid facing some of them altogether. In other ways hanging on to old behaviour patterns risks being an act of self-sabotage, or corporately, a hindrance to more enlightened paths to success. Better to set sail, with a combination of the right support and the right degree of challenge, than to hide from others – and more importantly oneself. Better not to miss the greater journey, albeit with some upheaval, for its potentially more exciting, empowering and joyous outcomes.

Communism cripples character: the story of how transition from political oppression to free democracy unleashed waves of innovation, capitalism, lies and laziness

Reflections for leaders

- What can we learn about leadership from this case study/observation?
- What is your relationship with authority – positive and/or negative examples?
- Which behaviours in Renata's account most interest you?
- What does this teach us about the leadership you may have experienced?

Reflections for coaches

- How can today's government leaders apply ideas from this case study?
- What can commercial sector leaders learn from Renata's story?
- What ideas does this case study offer public-sector leaders?
- What resonates for third-sector leaders?
- What learning does this story offer future leaders, who are currently at the beginning of their careers?

Note

1 Shibboleth: A custom or tradition, particularly through speech, which helps maintain segregation of in-group and an out-group. A construct to keep out threat.

References

Freud, S. (1940e). Splitting of the ego in the process of defence. S.E., 23:273-285.London: Hogarth Press.

Klein, M. (1960). www.melanie-Klein-trust.org.uk

Suggested reading

Kundera, M. (1992). *The Joke*. London: Faber & Faber (Original text written 1967).

Chapter 10

Comfort and containment

An exploration of the architectural and psychological 'spaces' associated with an experience of being in a neonatal intensive care unit

It's what 'space' you're in mentally, rather than the architecture per se, that determines your experience of a building. You might be moved from a crowded, grotty ward with building works going on . . . to a perfect new gleaming space, but it all depends on which space feels like 'home' for the patient. When our child was hospitalised, the old ward felt like home and therefore contained and comforted us better.

Dara Rigal BES MArch (Columbia), RIBA, ARB

Few people want to end up with a baby in neonatal intensive care (NICU). A place where expertise mingles with hope, thankfulness, desperation and often shock. This chapter is based on a poem I wrote in response to being the mother of a premature baby in NICU. The style of the poem is like a raw stream of emotion. I felt 'too tired' to write 'proper prose', even years later. This chapter represents an individual, deeply personal perspective. Yet the themes and ideas go beyond my own experiences and offer wider application about how spaces influence our thinking and what they represent.

The thoughts presented attempt to capture what is being expressed physically, emotionally and psychologically. It explores or indeed searches for the different kinds of 'spaces' in a neonatal intensive care unit. It asks what meaning and impact these have for those in the unit, either as patients, parents of neonates or staff.

The poem is divided into sections: Alarm, comfort and containment; noise, loss and conscious environment; EBM [expressed breast milk] and 'liquid gold'; the bus; and going home – from high dependency to healthy dependency.

After each section, a short analysis of the space is given, including comment on any conscious and unconscious processes which may be in play. The perspective of a nurse and an architect bring additional ideas and thoughts about the meaning of the different spaces in the unit.

Whilst this chapter focuses on the neonatal intensive care environment, the ideas and concepts analysed here are transferable to the working world generally. Leaders can begin to consider their personal 'architecture', that of their staff and that of their workspace, in terms of outcomes and performance. Coaches can work with clients to analyse literal and metaphorical spaces in connection to where and how they lead.

This chapter is based on an individual case study from a mother's point of view. The role of fathers is also imperative and encouraged in a neonatal context, although it is not explored here in depth.

Comfort and containment: an exploration of the architectural and psychological 'spaces' associated with an experience of being in a neonatal intensive care unit

Alarm, comfort and containment

POEM

Lights low, dark, hot, damp. Lines, drips and vitamin feeds. Oxygen masks and mattress alarms. Incubator. A small intimate space designed to recreate the womb. To gestate, bespoke and manage risk. A small, enclosed physical space. Comfort and containment.

Rolls of sheets and towels – oval nest around a miniature new-born. Babies born too small, too sick, too early. Adult hands touch head and buttocks, through flap windows in the incubator. Comfort and containment. Boundaries. UV tunnels over bare backed babies. Tiny nappies. Glossy floors.

Kangaroo Care. Skin-to-skin. Mother's chest heats the baby. Miracles of design. Voices singing. Comfort. Containment. Stress reduction. The brain is free to connect.

Boundaries. Limits. Limits to pain. Limits to suffering. Safe, intimate, constant. Warm spaces to relax. Spaces and smells where there are no heel pricks or procedures. Familiar voices. Already known in utero. Energy goes into growing instead of coping with stress. Comfort and containment. Positive association. The battle to survive, is converted into an opportunity to thrive.

Silent padding nurses. Rubber soled shoes. Yet an incubator is 16 times noisier than an average family home. No tapping the outside of this plastic box please. Lowered voices, lower stress for the baby. Incubator as a transitioning space – a space that is about emerging stronger. A transformational space. A living space, a *leaving space*.

Incubator babies and skin-to-skin

There are multiple spaces to consider in this short section of the poem. The incubator is a closed, dark space. It is kept wet to prevent the baby's skin from drying out. It is warm because this baby cannot yet regulate its own temperature. This is an acute emergency, where the risk of infection, hypothermia, internal bleeding and much else could kill a premature baby. The medical team tries to create a space for survival. Doctors attempt to stabilise the baby's heart beat and oxygen intake with the help of breathing apparatus, containment holding of the head and buttocks, and skin-to-skin contact with the parents whenever possible. The concept of containment refers to a human need for restriction, boundaries and the metaphorical 'holding' of distressing thoughts or emotions. Containment, both physically and psychologically, is comforting. It helps us feel calmer and more at peace. It helps us cope.

The surfaces in NICU are mostly hard, polished and wiped down daily. Even armchairs for parents to sit in and hold their babies need to be covered in faux leather plastic, to keep germs at bay. The incubator – a clear plastic box with a lid and a blanket covering the outside – tries to re-create a womb-like environment. For a number of reasons, the mother's womb may not have been able to 'contain' the baby any longer, hence a decision by mother nature or the medical team for the baby to be born. The incubator attempts to protect and contain.

Neonatal intensive care – a space specifically for new-born babies who are born too early, too sick or too small – is a high dependency space where both baby and parents' emotional states need to be proactively or consciously managed. Reducing the stress for the baby allows its energy to go into growing, breathing and thriving. UNICEF's 'family friendly/whole family care' initiative believes that by looking after the family unit holistically, babies make better progress developmentally. The spaces in NICU appear to be all about function. Creating protection, stabilising the temperature or humidity levels and minimising the risk of infection. Whilst simultaneously being ambitious for babies to be held close to their parent's skin, to enhance neural brain development and for emotional bonding on both sides to occur.

There are large spaces such as the ward, which sits within a large city teaching hospital. And there are minute spaces (Bachelard 1958) such as the nasogastric tube, drips and cannulas which are mere millimetres in diameter. Everything must be made smaller than usual, from diapers and hats to tiny strips of foam to shade the baby's eyes from the bright lights that the doctors need to carry out observations, brain scans or even operations inside the incubator. Within the unit sit several incubators, each linked up electronically to screens which monitor heart rate, breathing and medicine delivery.

Inside the incubator are further enclosing spaces – spaces within spaces. For example, a towel rolled into a sausage and shaped in an oval. This 'contains' or provides a physical boundary for the baby's legs and elbows to press against. To 'feel' a limit. To feel comforted. This physical device aims to offer emotional relief. Within the towelling oval is a tiny premature baby, whose organs are more miniature than normal term new-borns. Four chambers within the heart, the lungs – often not yet fully developed - offer more examples of internal spaces within the architecture of neonatal intensive care.

Physical or emotional stress triggers cortisol to be released in the brain. In contrast, loving, nurturing, safe, comforting, familiar smells, trigger a flood of oxytocin (the hormone which promotes a bonding, happy, contented, 'in love' state) to the baby's brain. Likewise, for the parents. And possibly, in parallel, for the medical teams caring for babies in a precarious state of health. So, the brain is another important space to consider when thinking about the impact of the environment on the emotional state and capacity to develop. We might apply this concept to other environments we live in or work in.

Whilst the baby gestates inside the incubator, its mother's womb (or gestational space) gradually contracts. In the case of a premature baby, the uterus is now no longer needed. It is a redundant space. A space from which a baby was delivered but a space which failed to hold onto the infant for the expected length of time. Here we have both the physical representation of a specific space but also a psychological metaphor around insufficiency, failure or rejection coming out of that physicality. This could mean rejection by the uterus of the baby or rejection of the uterus by the baby.

The psychological intention of neonatal intensive care

It could be assumed that doctors are solely concerned with physical survival, and thus their approach is purely physiological or anatomical. But the neonatal intensive care unit has a holistic, longer-term view, which represents more than the intention to promote life over death. From the first hours and days, there is an emphasis on healthy emotional as well as physical development.

Kangaroo Care is a part of this. The practice of holding an unclothed baby next to its mother or father's naked chest is also known as skin-to-skin contact. This physical space aims to provoke a familiar oxytocin or bonding state – an association with loving kindness and safety for the baby. Early recognition of familiar voices and smells is the early learning of who to trust and where reliable, consistent care can be found. In this intimate, warm, skin-to-skin space the baby is relaxed. Its oxygen saturation level goes up. Its heart rate stabilises. This is a happy space.

For this reason, when painful procedures are carried out, medical staff move the baby off its parent's chest, returning to skin-to-skin afterwards. This maintains the baby's trust in its safe space. I believe such conscious care given to establishing healthy attachments early in the baby's life contributes to faster physical and neural development in the short term and has the potential to promote good mental health in the longer term. With so much at stake at this delicate and fragile time, the more energy that goes into growing and developing, rather than into coping with stress, the better. I find the conscious integration of pharmaceutical medicine and psychological 'medicine' profound and impressive.

An exclusive and excluding space

The intensive care space has much to offer our creativity and imagination, in terms of looking below the surface. Most people will never see inside a neonatal intensive care unit. They would not be allowed in. Such is the risk of infection that during the 'flu season' grandparents and even siblings are barred from seeing the new-born in their family. NICU becomes an excluding space. A space where segregation occurs according to role, family position and status.

During staff shift changes, not even the baby's parents are allowed in the unit. The reason for this is anchored in respect for patient privacy. Even with such tiny neonates, you won't hear about the health condition of the baby next to yours, nor vice versa.

So, NICU is an *exclusive* space. You have to be 'special' to be allowed in here. Many who are in here wish they were not, in fact, so special. They would prefer to be at home with a healthy baby of course. Few people would want to belong to such an exclusive club. This is a high risk space. Such is the preoccupation with infection that washing hands and sterilising equipment is repeated throughout the day by everyone on the unit. One could argue that NICU is a neurotic space. More than one nurse in NICU uttered:

> *You don't have to be OCD [obsessive compulsive disorder] to work here, but it helps!*

Whilst the neonatal intensive care unit tries to encourage Kangaroo Care, parents cannot live at the hospital, although they are welcome to visit, day or night. At first, some babies are too fragile to leave their incubator for long. Many have tubes, oxygen equipment and electronic sensors attached to their feet. This apparatus 'interrupts' what Winnicott calls the 'nursing couple' (Winnicott 1940) – his notion that in the normal state there is no baby as such, because mother-and-baby are like an inseparable or merged couple. The father is temporarily excluded, whilst nature's animal instincts take over and refuse to allow anyone between mother and child. When this is successful, both parent and child experience the unit as an oxytocin space. This is a space where the foundations of a capacity for empathy and emotional connection are laid, a sort of natural 'neonatal intensive care'.

In NICU the 'nursing couple' is almost inevitably interrupted and disrupted. So NICU can be a separating space. A great deal is done to try to re-establish connection and deep bonding, with both parents, not just the mother. This investment not only promotes immediate wellbeing, but also has important long-term implications for the empathic health of the baby as it develops through childhood and into adulthood.

Spatial constructs – the nurse and the architect

> *I know this hospital probably looks old and falling apart and covered in pigeon droppings . . . but inside this unit, it's clean and we'll do the very best we can for your baby.*
>
> **Nurse**

> *People can take the same space and transform it. Space is about who the people are and how they make that space for others. You can have a gleaming glass and steel ward that looks luxurious like a spa, but the old, decaying ward may be 'home' for you in hospital. History gives meaning too. Space is not just physical, it's security, how you were cared for in that space . . . it's the work what goes on inside it.*
>
> **Architect**

A nurse's perspective

I asked a nurse how it feels to be one of the medical team, caring for babies on the neonatal intensive care unit. How do medics cope with the levels of stress attached to their jobs, including dealing with the distress of parents?

> *Many parents say their baby is in the 'best place'. We are trying to replicate the womb but a plastic box with a blanket over it isn't that. I think of what we're putting families through. Fertility is meant to be about blossoming and growing, but lots of couples end up in our care because of infertility, which if they have IVF treatment, makes them more likely to have twins, or other complications which increase the risk of ending up in NICU. Even though parents don't want to be here, they are alleviated of their intense anxiety. They hand it over to the ward staff.*

So NICU offers some degree of containment for parental angst, as babies fight for life. The unit acts as a vessel to receive babies who cannot be looked after by their parents in the community. Some staff feel the level of care they offer is not enough:

> *As a nurse you feel less anxious than a parent even though you heart is breaking. But in the architectural sense NICU is not a home, it's not where you want to be. The warmth is artificial warmth, it's medicalised, it's inhuman. On the unit it's all about medical devices to keep babies alive. Just reflecting on that makes me think that we don't focus on the human enough.*

Maybe this applies also to the wellbeing of the medical staff. Isabell Menzies Lyth talks about the effect of stressful and distressing work, specifically of dealing with pain, on nurses. Her study of an adult ward observed how nurses split up tasks, so for example one did a bed bath, another administered medicine. Nobody treated the 'whole person'. Indeed, patients were often referred to as Bed 2 or 'the liver in bed 6', rather than by their names (Menzies Lyth 1960). She called this 'splitting'. Splitting off from the pain aroused in medical staff by sick patients. This includes splitting off from the pain a nurse may cause a patient in the course of offering them treatment which ultimately helps them recover.

Splitting can occur in many professions, not just medicine. We may even resort to it in our home lives. It is a defence against what is unbearable. Professionally it is a way of dealing with emotional overload without burning out, taking sick time or not being able to face coming to work. Splitting is particularly prevalent in jobs like the fire service, the police or the armed forces, or other occupations which bring a person into deep connection with another, for example teaching, psychotherapy or leading a religious community. This defence may be an effective temporary coping mechanism. But it has its risks if used long term. Aspects of splitting can become culturally or institutionally embedded without anyone realising. Such behaviour or practices can compromise the wellbeing of staff, their performance at work and even the sustainability of their organisation.

An architect's perspective

Architect Dara Rigal examines the incubator from an architectural perspective:

> *The incubator space is about transparency. Doctors need to be able to see the baby and respond to its needs, whilst wanting at the same time to create a warm, stable, darkened environment which is less stressful for the neonate.*
>
> *With its giraffe neck lift-up lid and four hand-hole windows, the incubator certainly allows access. But its transparency is the biggest obstacle to contact around. The same concept applies to the current trend for steel and glass offices or apartment blocks. Transparency can make people go inside their heads, in search of private space when their environment is so exposed. People separate themselves from others in order to find 'space' or time out from total transparency. Transparency and being so exposed is dehumanising.*

The furniture of NICU includes masks, funnels and tubes, computer screens and monitors. These illustrate the heartbeat, which can be psychologically comforting but does not offer any tactile comfort. It is all hard surfaces and flashing numbers. However, skin-to-skin holding does give a soft, warm, tactile experience to both baby and parent. As we know it attempts to mitigate some of the risk of the emotional disconnect, distrust or trauma by instead creating associations of safety, security and empathy:

> *Arguably, the more all of us connect to spaces around us, our environment, our cities, the more 'healing' can take place. The more empathy people can develop between each other.*
>
> [Architect]

Another item of furniture in NICU is a chest of drawers containing crocheted blankets and miniature cardigans and hats. On one occasion leading up to Christmas, a knitted nativity scene was arranged on the top of it. This speaks to the architecture of the community, which surrounds the neonatal intensive care unit. Teams of volunteer knitters cannot access the inside of the unit, but they can communicate that they are thinking about what goes on inside it. Nurses knitting on their days off speaks to the commitment felt by some of those who are allowed inside NICU. This also tells us of the commitment but perhaps also of the failure of some staff to successfully cut off from work on a rest day.

Whether staff or volunteers, knitters must use polyester yarn because all items are washed at 60 degrees centigrade. Again, even something attempting tactile comfort and warmth must meet the stringent standards of cleanliness. Blankets covering the outside of the incubators or tiny clothes for the babies inside them may be more about protecting the internal architecture of the parents. It is something for them to touch. Perhaps to trigger an oxytocin state, within an emotionally hard experience. This has the possibility to reconnect the parent with being wrapped up in a blanket and cared for as a baby themselves. It may enhance the parent's desire to care for their baby, something the medical staff constantly keeps an eye on.

The chest of drawers containing the tiny knitted clothes stands at the end of a narrow corridor. The corridors provide access routes to the babies. They also act as an unintended channel of communication, says Dara Rigal:

> *Because the corridors are narrow, they can cause conversations to happen. Rather than needing an appointment with your baby's consultant, you are likely to bump into them. And them with you. So, corridors are a device for informal meetings. They enable a flow of conversation between parents and doctors.*

Noise, loss and conscious environment

POEM

Fresh clean shirts. Washed hair. Hand scrubbing. In an environment brought about by fertility, the goal is now, sterility. There is annihilation anxiety. Consultants and nurses counsel and console families. Staff may feel traumatised too. Emitting calm. Trust. Truthful exchange. Or as near to truth as can be tolerated on both sides. Measured positivity. Everyone is conscious of potential loss and heartbreak. How much dare I emotionally invest in this threatened life? Who am I as a person? Not the selfless, able, strong one you'd like to think I might be. A door almost wrenched off its hinges, swinging in a bleak, abandoned outback. Tendons not strong enough. A parent's heart . . . pumping with adrenaline . . . a small, muscular space, flooded with angst.

Client centred respect. Tiny patients. Staggering vulnerability. Whole family care philosophy. Promoters of growth. Dark, warm, damp; eyes shielded from the light. A heated mattress. Incubators covered by the efforts of volunteer knitters. Darkness, stillness. A conscious replication of safety. Comfort and containment. The institution tries to create an intimate environment.

Nurses choosing childlessness. Woken by alarms in their dreams. Not their biological clock. But by concern: *'Are my babies OK?'* Broken attachments when babies die; broken attachments when they thrive and, along with their parents, leave the unit.

Nurses teaching doctors. An addictive incapacity to relax. Highest purpose, leaders in the field. How do those dealing with pain at work, handle their own pain? Can you switch off this kind of intensity? What parts of the person or the organisation – the National Health Service (NHS) – may also need intensive care?

Managing physical and emotional suffering

Again, here we see the physical spaces within the body – the heart, the brain – referred to in terms of vulnerability and the overwhelm of emotional stress or 'flooding' which occurs. Including when outside the hospital an alarm sounds, setting off feelings of emergency or catastrophe by association. The physicality of the hospital environment is emphasised again – the mattress, the washing of hands, the knitting. Also mentioned is the psychological concept of attachment. Together with the fear of loss, or broken attachments caused by death. Even on their days off, some nurses appear to evidence difficulty in detaching from their worry or concern for the babies in their care. At other times, medical staff may need to sever attachment, lest they become too anxious to perform the tasks expected of them in their job.

Some nurses explicitly express deciding not to have children, because of what they see every day on the neonatal intensive care ward. Others find they can't detach, such is the intensity and also the sense of professional meaning and reward from being part of the NICU medical team.

Both staff and families on the ward need mechanisms to release the fear and tension they are going through. We see parents making jokes or generating humorous euphemisms about what's going on. For example, referring to a stomach or intestinal reflux drug 'domperidone' as 'baby champagne' – a reference to the French champagne brand Dom Perignon. Humour can be a coping mechanism. A distancing device.

Another distancing device can be 'depersonalising' the patient (Menzies 1960). Medical staff might resort to this in order to manage pity, compassion, love, guilt, resentment and even envy at the level of care patients receive compared to how hard the medical staff are working and/or the way in which staff are cared for by managers, provoked by coming to work in NICU. Depersonalising equates to the denial of the whole person.

Compared to in the past, today's neonatal units try to support staff to integrate their feelings, rather than split off from the emotions evoked by their tiny patients. One nurse is usually charged with several babies rather than merely certain tasks associated with one baby or another. Babies are referred to as babies or by their name, rather than their cot number. This may be a 'healthier' approach but systemically, it could also be harder emotionally on medical staff when things go wrong.

As previously mentioned, the medical teams must manage the physical suffering and emotional experience of not just their patient, but its family. Family members may feel *'like a door wrenched off its hinges'* – stretched beyond their capacity to cope, be that physically or emotionally. Many families have other children to care for at home or must accommodate certain cultural demands, e.g. cooking and cleaning for the in-laws, before coming to the hospital.

Mum, who is still recovering from giving birth may experience medical complications or loss of confidence or capacity to breastfeed. Simultaneously, partners try to juggle going to work with coming to the hospital daily or twice daily. Some fathers voice that they have not had time to cry because they are so worried about their baby, its mother and holding down their job.

The architect and the nurse

The nurse

> *NICU has the highest sickness rate in the hospital. We have the highest staff turnover. It's not real sickness, it's* the *stress of the job, stress of management and the stress of having little formal psychological support,' says one nurse. 'I never resent a baby for being ill and making me feel its pain. I resent my system for the processes and politics of the work and the job.*
>
> *Sometimes you can fix a baby but the emotion of the family is unmanageable, especially for junior nurses who tend to take everything personally. If a nurse thinks they've done something wrong, they go off sick the next day. But they're not sick. I call them 'mental health days', which is why we match junior staff with a more senior person, so one person isn't shouldering all of the burden.*

The pairing up nurses represents a shift from sole to collective responsibility. So systemically, we do see some form of splitting going on, but it is part of a conscious strategy to promote psychological health and staff retention. I call it 'paired integration'. It helps junior nurses in particular cope with their feelings of responsibility and distress in this high intensity, high risk environment.

The architect

For doctors and nurses, repetitive handwashing and the changing of disposable plastic aprons after every contact with a baby is an accepted and necessary part of the job. It is also incumbent upon parents to cooperate with the rules of a sterile environment. From an architect's point of view, this compulsory routine around cleanliness offers an additional interpretation or meaning-making:

> *Washing your hands at the sink as you enter NICU is about ceremonies, ritual and setting the rhythm of the day as you arrive to see your baby. It's like a moment of mindfulness amidst the trauma.*

Handwashing may also feel like a barrier for medical staff rushing to respond to a baby in distress. Similarly, for parents desperate to reconnect with a baby in a critical condition, whom they feared may not survive the night. Underneath this urgent desire to 'reach' their baby could be an indicator of healthy bonding; a need to comfort the baby or a need to comfort oneself, having been separated overnight.

As we know, in a 'normal' new-born context, parents have constant access to their baby as they go about household tasks or going to the shops. There is usually no enforced separation. The parents room is a cross between a communal lounge and a student kitchen. It is an attempt to offer some respite and home comforts such as a sofa, a television and a microwave. Dara Rigal:

> *This is a place of discussion, sharing, not wanting to share and/or not wanting to hear stories of sick children. The parents room is a place of community, of comfort. Or not.*

Systemically, the parents room may be a place to contain emotional angst or exhaustion, away from the ward. With other parents sitting in there, also in distress and shock, it may actually offer no respite at all. On a practical level, the parents room is a place to go during staff shift handover. This is the only time in 24 hours when parents are not permitted to be on the ward. The parents room may be a place to rest, away from the stressful beeping of machines and alarms on the unit. For staff, it may offer a degree of respite from 'containing' the distress of parents with a child in NICU.

EBM and 'liquid gold'

POEM

> EBM: Expressed Breast Milk – considered 'liquid gold' by the doctors; a uniquely valuable medicine only nature can supply. This is important work. A collapse of dreamy notions of nurture and love. But an act of love it certainly must be. Or at least, a crude indicator of a primitive bond. A bond one fears to make.
>
> EBM. Big space. No baby. No triggers for milk flow. Instead, machines and plastic funnels and hygiene angst. Breastfeeding into a tube. Big space, no baby. Pain. Sore. Motivated by medical imperative. Urgency. Emergency. Only one person can do this. One person on earth. [Donated EMB is pasteurised so a degree of benefit is lost].
>
> Kangaroo Care and a conversation with a nurse, prompt a milk response so strong, it wakes me to pump at 3am. The power of a conversation to improve physiological outcomes. Prevents depression. Conversation. Comfort. Anxiety containment. Optimism creation. Lifesaving results. The breast is full to overflowing. Richness and fat pours onto an emotionally exhausted landscape.

Euphemism and humour: attempted escape from high anxiety

The Dairy. EBM Central. The Espresso Bar & Chill. The Pump Room 'n' Spa. Euphemism and humour used by mothers in the hospital's expressing room. Attempts at fun in crisis but no one is truly laughing. Nor convinced by reassurance. Attempts at containment only work up to a point; the raw, wild, primitive rage and call for life, quivers beneath the surface of civility.

Fear and loss intermingle. Fear of attachment. Fear amongst the medical staff of parental attachment failing to form. Architects, broadcasters, call-centre workers, immigrant and refugee mothers. All expressing milk to help their babies survive. The plastic chairs are uncomfortable. A nylon curtain wafts in the breeze. Breaths of fresh air from the outside world enter the unit through barred windows of mottled, shatterproof glass. A hint that this space was historically intended for a different use.

Pumping milk every two hours causes blistering and pain. Repeated pain. Repeated masochism. Yet this buttery, golden-coloured goodness is an exclusive, prized resource. It is gratefully received by a whole family of doctors, nurses and relatives. But expressing, like breastfeeding, is tiring. A woman burns up to 500 calories every 24 hours. How hard do you have to run in a gym to achieve that?

Expressing is remote feeding. It feels far from the imagined warmth and softness of the normal mother-to-baby connection. 'Normal' being the imagined arrival into motherhood: The fantasy of a confident breastfeeding regime, peaceful walks through parks and woodland, the bounce of celebration, indulgence and enjoyment. Instead, living in NICU, this is a brutally different beginning of life. Or death. One doesn't know which.

The intensive care experience is an exercise in presence. In living in the now. There is no visible future. Few are safe enough to relax. You don't have to look far to find an even more serious case than one's own. Instead of standard infant milestones, there are tiny celebrations of positive progress along the journey that can be a marathon of hope and despair.

The business of skin-to-skin containment holding, expressing milk and commuting to and from the hospital, sees 10 hours pass as one. Because of the risk of contamination and the need for isolation from the outside world, parents develop a vibrant, empathic and energising community of nursing and consultant teams, which rotate around the clock. There is much mutual respect and admiration.

Sometimes after months of expressing, the baby's suck, swallow and remember-to-breathe reflexes synchronise. Direct breastfeeding is now possible. Tears of joy stream down faces as staff and strangers witness this first intimate, mother-to-baby exchange. A close, closed, exclusive space, experienced in the dark and the heat of neonatal intensive care. Here is the reward for the pain, angst and self-discipline. Oxytocin shines its magic light on both mother and child. Theirs is a co-dependency, the milk a co-created resource. Triggers of life. Feeding tires the baby, who rests then, recharged, calls out for more. The child is launched. Launched for independence from the High Dependency Unit. From high dependency, to healthy dependency.

The architect's perspective

Expressing milk in public could be considered exposing or even undignified. It is certainly disconnected to what one normally expects in terms of the experience of feeding a baby. Whilst in another setting one might introduce comfy chairs and soft curtains, in hospital, everything must have wiped clean, non-porous surfaces. Milk funnels are washed and expressed milk put in a communal, unlocked fridge. Every surface is hard. Every surface is cold. Every surface is sterilised.

The fridge used to store expressed breast milk, or to defrost frozen EBM (expressed breast milk), is yet another machine. Again, its sharp-edged, steel surfaces emphasise the clash of clinical mechanisation with the notion of gently nurturing a child.

From a psychological perspective, this industrial, hospital fridge represents both risk and trust. There is a risk associated with allowing parents to open and close a massive temperature-controlled fridge, full of medication, as well as precious expressed breast milk. There is also a risk that should the refrigerator malfunction and its temperature rise, the milk inside it would no longer be safe to use. It would have to be thrown away. Another element of risk and trust, which it would appear nobody questions, is the possibility of parents stealing or contaminating cultures of another baby's milk. A subtle watch is kept by the head nurse in charge.

An unseen or 'invisible' space is the NICU freezer. This is used to store excess EBM – a spare resource to call upon if the mother's milk dries up or if she has overproduced and the baby is too small or too ill to be given it yet. The milk bank also contains donated EBM. Donated milk must be pasteurised and screened for numerous diseases including hepatitis and HIV, so it lacks some of the nutritional content of unpasteurised breast milk. Nevertheless, it is a highly valued resource.

Whatever its origin, every bottle of EBM is carefully labelled and dated. Literally not a drop is wasted. The attention to waste may be part of the unit's conscious psychological care of the mother. To keep encouraging milk generation, for immediate use but also for the medium and longer term when, hopefully, the baby is home and thriving and continuing to be breast fed. It recognises the effort and self-discipline involved.

Whilst mothers may leave the ward to express milk in the expressing room, doctors and nurses may seek respite in the staff room. The windows are too high to be able to see through them. This design is unlikely to be by chance. The doors are solid and always closed. There is probably much to contain in this non-public space, says architect Dara Rigal:

> *It's a barrier, away from parents where the unsaid can be shared between staff. It's also probably witness to a variety of coping behaviours from emotional unloading and talking things through, to draining a can of diet coke or a strong cup of coffee; it's a place to grab a packet of cigarettes before heading outside for a discreet cigarette. The staff room may house or contain the staff in some way, but there may be plenty between staff that's also not said.*

As mentioned earlier in this chapter, the mother's uterus is now redundant and continues to retract. The act of breastfeeding, including expressing, helps this process. As the baby grows larger inside the incubator, its mother's in-built incubator grows smaller. Is the mother *becoming less?* The uterus and the incubator are both gestational spaces, designed for thriving, transformation and ultimately leaving. As the baby learns to thrive on breast milk or a combination of breast milk and powdered formula milk, we transfer our attention from internal, uterine spaces to external spaces like an open cot. Parents may even begin to allow themselves to fantasise about other external spaces such as the park or home; their cautious hopes that their baby is gradually growing stronger and may eventually leave NICU begin to creep into their consciousness. The parents' fantasy concerns not only health, but separation from their baby. The next part of this chapter considers the journey to and from the neonatal intensive care unit.

The bus

POEM

> An umbilical cord between home and hospital. Ordinary life cruelly continues oblivious to your critical situation. Isn't that every passenger's story? Anonymity. Nobody knows why *you're* on the bus. The bus. A space. A cavity where many unknown stories sit next to each other. Passengers transiting through, to and from and with their pain. Banality may offer some relief from it. The bus. What will hit me on arrival? What am I leaving behind when I go home?
>
> Local restaurants flourish. Normal families enjoying themselves. I feel envy. I'm not here to enjoy my meal. I'm here to eat one. Separation anxiety of being away from the unit. At home I'm too tired to speak, too tired to listen to a message on the answer machine. One's only function is to return to the ward in the morning. Hard and hardening. But harder still when there are more children at home to bring up. Or a job to hold down, a business to run. Splitting. Simultaneous needs in multiple locations.

Cords of connection, nourishment and commuting

The bus is a vital link with the hospital. It is a transitional space. A decompression zone. This connection with the neonatal unit need not be a bus; it could equally be a car, a taxi, a train or the telephone. The bus as a mode of transport, a cavity like the uterus. It delivers the parents to NICU each day. It represents the method of reconnection with the baby and also of detachment or separation from the baby, when its parents go home each evening to sleep.

Consider the design of the bus: It is a transparent, rectangular box on wheels, with windows and doors to allow entry and exit. Like an incubator, it is also a see-through box, on wheels, with doors and windows to allow access and travel.

But only one of these vehicles can bring a baby home from hospital. Arguably the whole purpose of the incubator is ultimately also to bring the baby home. It is a vehicle designed to promote flourishing. To deliver optimal care within the hospital or hospital network setting. Then to move the baby through various stages of development, from high dependency to being healthy enough to leave hospital in its parent's arms. Or as the law would have it in some countries, in a cushioned baby seat, suitable for travel.

All the while Mum is still expressing milk or breastfeeding directly. As we know, breastfeeding burns calories. So, mothers must eat plenty of protein. Whilst in some cultures parents are well nourished, with both grandmothers flying into intensive catering mode, other couples' or indeed single parents' circumstances mean they must manage with much less practical support.

Restaurants inside the hospital offer basic hot food and snacks. In the restaurants outside the hospital, life appears to carry on, oblivious to the pain of those dipping in and out of the acute medical setting nearby. There is much on the mind of a NICU parent buying themselves a meal whether inside or outside the hospital setting.

Going home

POEM

> EMB[1] fridge. EMB bank. New freezer at home. Emptied freezer at home. Emptied breast. Mother's drawn face. Fat from a 6-month pregnancy used up. Fat from a 9-month pregnancy, never accumulated. No remaining resource. The food source is running dry. We're into brand named formula from a factory. Annihilation anxiety if it runs out. Only on prescription at the chemist.[2] One day we didn't need any more. Moving to normal. From special care, concerned, anxious . . . to normal. A space where there *is* resource. Emotions steady. Used to medical structures and support. Now no institution. Free-fall. Normal. Immense responsibility. The couple is now 'alone' with their baby. Some friends fear to come near.

From high dependency to healthy dependency

At this point the mother is not only exhausted from the trauma of the baby's arrival, but she is also concerned about the literal exhaustion of her milk supply. Understandably it is more challenging to generate good quality breast milk under stressful conditions, such as war, famine, domestic violence or a premature birth context.

This part of the poem tells of the fear that the precious, indeed life-giving and life-enhancing medicine that is breast milk may be running out. Also, the fear that special prescription-only premature formula milk powder may also run out. The fear is about not being able to nourish the child. Standard milk formula can usually be obtained at almost any time of day or night.

Fear that the resource may run out could be linked to an unconscious fear that there won't be enough *love*. Or enough emotional resource to keep coping now that the baby is out of hospital and its parents must let go of the institution. The concept of weaning the parents off medical support enters our thinking here as we consider whether it is the parents who are now in a high-dependency state, rather than their child.

The sense of free-fall is probably felt by most parents bringing a new-born baby home, wondering how on earth they will manage to look after it. Such natural fears are magnified when the NICU history is taken into account. The concept of 'well enough to go home' does not equal a status of being entirely without health worries for a baby born too early, too sick or too small.

Parents, especially first-time parents, may not know what 'healthy' dependency or healthy per se looks like. This is hardly surprising as for these parents, the journey to hospital to give birth has taken the form of multiple housings before coming home, from the labour suite to intensive care. Then promotion from Level 3 intensive care to the lower Level 2 or 1. After NICU to the Special Care Baby Unit (SCBU), then as oxygen supplies, mattress alarms and oxygen saturation monitors are stripped away, 'rooming in' is offered. This means a couple of nights' stay in the equivalent of a hospital hotel room, with the baby, but without medical treatment.

The nursing station is just a few metres away. The parents are left alone behind closed doors to look after the baby. This includes during the day and overnight, in preparation for going home. As goodbyes are said, a significant ending is acknowledged. Staff and parents attempt to end their attachment to each other and in the case of the parents, to the unit.

Seeing doctors and nurses make a special effort to say goodbye signifies not just professionalism but also a conscious handling of endings, which parents may not be aware of. This has not been a transaction of healthcare. It has been a journey of transition, growth, transformation and bonding. It has been a longer 'delivery' than originally anticipated.

In the case of an unhappy outcome, rituals of saying goodbye are also carried out, in an attempt to appropriately manage the trauma and grieving process of a different kind of ending.

Excluded spaces – the nursery, the isolation ward and the hospital mortuary

There are three spaces this chapter has not considered in depth: The nursery, the isolation ward and the hospital mortuary.

The nursery – the baby's bedroom or cot at home – may be a space prepared in happy anticipation of the arrival of a healthy baby. If the baby is stillborn or dies in hospital, this space sits cruelly empty. A receptacle never filled. In the case of a premature baby, the nursery may still be a home-office; such was the nature of the sudden, unanticipated arrival. There may be no baby equipment or cot in the home at all.

The isolation ward is used when a baby is transferred from another hospital, is known to harbour infection or to be at particular risk of catching an infection. It is a space within the NICU space. A small ward, away from other parents and babies. This exclusive and excluding room is a yet higher level of defence against anxiety and contamination. It represents a two-way fear. After an appropriate time of apartheid, the baby is usually welcomed to the rest of the ward, into the broader NICU community. Of course, isolation for a baby means isolation for its parents and also for the staff assigned to look after it.

In other cases, a baby has no visitors anyway. It is cared for with absolute discretion by the nursing staff, ahead of adoption. There are some gentle dawnings and painful realisations as an observer on NICU: One is sometimes an observer of the unsaid.

The hospital mortuary may not be a space in the conscious awareness of parents with a baby in NICU. Death is front of mind, yes. But not the mortuary. The hospital mortuary is usually in the basement. The lowest you can go . . . beneath the conscious . . . or stored somewhere aiming to be inaccessible or psychologically out of reach. The mortuary represents a highly feared destination. So feared it is invisible. The unconscious lack of awareness of its existence by parents may represent a primal preoccupation with survival and life. A rage to exist. Such are the enormous efforts, energies and resources that go into the preservation of life, be that in a medical, cultural or spiritual context. This includes the instinct to protect one's child from death.

Spiritual assistance along the way

Whilst the primary focus of the staff in NICU is on medical intervention, we have seen throughout this chapter how almost equal value is given to the emotional wellbeing of both the baby and its parents, in service of better health outcomes for the baby. Included in this, where desired by the parents, is attention to the spiritual needs or beliefs of the baby's family.

The hospital chaplain may be called to visit Christian families. When it is Ramadan or Eid, there is a sense of it on the unit. Rabbis are occasionally seen naming an incubator baby on its eight day. [The Jewish tradition for male circumcision cannot be performed at this time as would usually be the case for a healthy child.] In Ugandan culture it is usual for many different family members to choose a name for the baby. So, grandma chooses a name; favourite uncles, aunts and siblings add their choices also. I watched as one baby in NICU was given 18 names by his priest, in the presence of his parents and the other patients on the unit.

So, whilst we can assume the neonatal intensive care ward is preoccupied with science-based medical and psychological care, there is definitely space allocated for spiritual belief. This aligns with the unit's 'whole family care' philosophy. It acknowledges the potential of a variety of inputs to enhance wellbeing and outcomes.

This chapter has explored attachment on the unit and to the unit. Can one ever leave this space? Do the experiences on a neonatal intensive care ward ever leave those involved? Good memories and well-handled messages can mean that in some ways one does not leave or seek to leave the NICU space. When the baby and its parents return home, they hold on to or associate the unit with having had a 'good' experience within this particularly difficult context.

Many families return some months later to show off the baby and reconnect with their favourite nurses, consultant pediatricians or receptionist. Some hospitals have an annual party and fundraiser. This optional invitation is a mechanism for maintaining positive links with the unit rather than severing them forever.

Some parents return to NICU as parent volunteers, supporting distressed families going through similar experiences to their own. Becoming a volunteer – ideally in a professionally supervised context – may offer that person a profound and ongoing chord of connection back to the unit that helped them and their child. Other families become fundraisers. Others donate expressed breast milk.

Upsetting experiences or inappropriate handling of a situation by staff can also make 'leaving' NICU either imperative or difficult – psychologically banked as unforgettable additions to the trauma of having a baby in intensive care. Some families avoid engaging with the unit from the moment they leave it, splitting off from the emotional pain associated with it. However this can also occur in families who have had a positive experience on the unit. Many parents 'forget' or deny aspects of their experience on the unit altogether.

This chapter has already highlighted the risk of overwhelm for staff. For them, extra sick days (referred to earlier as 'mental health days') and burn out represent ways of 'leaving' the unit either temporarily or permanently. Staff who come in on their days off or knit for the unit at home after their shift has ended offer us evidence that it is not always easy to leave the unit, or for the effects of neonatal intensive care to leave *you*. Staff may need a spiritual, sporting or other outlet too.

Closing thoughts

This chapter invites you into an exclusive space. With a bias towards a mother's perspective, it acknowledges the importance of both parents' feelings, role and contribution towards positive outcomes and the wellbeing of a child in NICU and beyond. We can see how very many questions, positive associations and anxieties arise, in response to the nature of the spaces in a neonatal intensive care ward. Some questions cannot be answered. Some cannot perhaps, be asked. There is much transference and counter transference over the days, weeks or months, whilst a baby is in the care of the unit as heightened emotions are processed.

Through a poem and subsequent analysis of the text, some of the physical, metaphorical and architectural spaces within a neonatal intensive care context are explored. Psychoanalytic insights are offered alongside interpretations of these literal spaces, for example, the incubator, the bus and the chambers of the heart. Concepts such as high dependency, uterine contraction or redundancy and the importance of the breast as a resource are discussed. In addition, the idea of the 'nursing couple' – the mother and baby bond which is interrupted by the imperative for incubation, oxygen tubes, drips, lines and nasogastric tubes. Long-term flourishing and the capacity for empathy is thought to be linked to some of these concepts.

The stress experienced by medical staff caring for babies in a critical state of health is also explored. The perspectives of a nurse and an architect add to our understanding and interpretation of what it is like living and working in NICU.

This chapter also touches upon some unacknowledged spaces such as the empty nursery at home and the hospital mortuary. It also questions whether there is space for spirituality in NICU. The concept of whole family care is connected to treating each patient, i.e. the new-born baby and its parents, in an integrated way. That includes their work, home and any cultural contexts.

The application of this chapter for leaders and coaches

For the imaginative leader there is plenty to borrow from this chapter about neonatal intensive care, in terms of how to spot and think about spaces in the workplace. Not just how architecture and interior design affects how people feel and function, but in terms of investigating the metaphorical and psychological spaces which may be at play, either consciously or unconsciously, whilst people work.

When is anxiety contained for employees and when do leaders attempt but fail or even refuse to contain anxiety? Consider the impact of how endings are handled at work. When there is hope, fear, denial, 'death' of some sort, e.g. redundancy or an organisational restructure. Consider also a multi-lens approach: individual experiences or patterns of behaviour in employees may represent something systemic that's going on but has not consciously been noticed.

Concepts from a neonatal context can be translated for a commercial or other business context such as boundaries and containment, the incubation of ideas in a start-up company for example, the creation of a sterile or a fertile thinking environment. The cleanliness required in a hospital environment may echo health and safety considerations on an oil rig, in a restaurant setting or in a primary school. It is important to consider aspects of exposure, noise, light levels, walls and textures in relation to the potential stress these may generate in some employees. Also, to ask what behaviours or spatial arrangements trigger cortisol (stress) or oxytocin (bonding, happy, contented) states and, subsequently, influence outcomes. This applies to oneself as a leader and those one is leading.

Consider the concepts of the uterus, the nursery and the mortuary. Which other parts of our lives or ourselves represent beginnings and endings? The juxtaposition of possibility and potential, versus the finite or the irreversible?

I believe the concept of 'spaces', with the help of the many examples of below the surface thinking explored in this chapter, can be applied across disciplines, from health to teaching to shipping, electronics, retail and banking.

Post script

I gave a talk based on this chapter at an international conference of psychoanalysts, organisational consultants and leadership coaches. One member of the audience yawned, then clearly felt embarrassed that I had spotted this, and later expressed that he felt overwhelmed by the experiences described within the neonatal intensive care experience. Another person clutched her skull with her hands, saying 'it was too much for her brain to cope with'. On recounting how the talk was received to the neonatal nurse featured in the text, she said:

> *Premature babies have fewer cues than babies born at term, to let their carers [parents and medical staff] know how they are feeling. When premature babies are overwhelmed, overstimulated or becoming tired from being held or from medical intervention, they yawn, or move their hands to cover their face.*

I thought it worth sharing how the reactions of these two conference delegates equated so similarly to the responses of a premature baby in an incubator. Thinking psychoanalytically, one would not consider this a coincidence.

Comfort and containment: an exploration of the architectural and psychological 'spaces' associated with an experience of being in a neonatal intensive care unit

Reflections for leaders

- What reactions did you notice yourself having in response to this chapter?
- Where are the trusted spaces in your workplace?
- What boundaries offer containment to your staff?
- Where do you as a leader experience fear and risk?
- How might a trauma or significant event you have experienced, either work related or home related, inform the way you lead?
- How might this difficult experience hold you back?
- How could you leverage it such that the trauma or struggle enhances the quality of your leadership?
- What 'spaces' do you find difficult or impossible to leave or re-enter?
- What could this tell you about the organisation rather than just about an individual?

Reflections for coaches

- The nature of the spaces for this leader – the spaces they operate in, the spaces they create for others
- From reading this chapter what are you now conscious of?
- What may be uncomfortable and in the subconscious, that requires exploring?
- Where are the umbilical cords in this system or within this leader?
- What about for their coach?

Thanks and dedication

To the hospital staff and expert practitioners – from cleaners, porters, ambulance drivers and incubator transfer teams to student nurses, nurses, registrars, consultants, psychotherapists and occupational therapists: people who work day and night in service of the survival and flourishing of others.

To my husband, who carried us with dedication, tenderness and care.

Notes

1 Expressed Breast Milk.
2 The chemist held an emergency spare for me just in case, but never told me.

References

Bachelard, G. (1958). *The Poetics of Space*. New York: Penguin (p. 149 and p. 167).

Menzies Lyth, I. (1960). Social systems as a defence against anxiety: An empirical study of the nursing service of a general hospital. *Human Relations*, 13, 95–121.

Winnicott, D.W. (1960). The theory of the parent-infant relationship. *The International Journal for Psychoanalysis*, 41:585–95.

Suggested reading

Lazar, R., Ropke, C. and Ermann, G. (1998, October). Learning to be: On the observation of a premature baby. *The International Journal of Infant Observation*, 2(1). Tavistock Clinic Foundation. ISSN 13698036

Obholzer, A. and Zagier Roberts, V. (1994). *The Unconscious at Work: Individual and Organisational Stress in the Human Services*. London & New York: Routledge.

Chapter 11

Closing thoughts

This book has brought fresh, unique and applicable research to the field of leadership development and coaching. Each case study has brought rigour and challenge. From sport to humanitarian aid, from supermarkets to medicine to prisons.

The leaders interviewed, many of whom are former coaching clients, give passionate and insightful accounts of their organisations and working environments. Inspiringly, these leaders communicated not just the stress derived from doing complex and sometimes dangerous jobs, but also the satisfaction, inner growth and the fun as well. In other cases, contributors offered deep observations of the impacts of different kinds of leadership or responses evoked by a particular environment.

Most chapters focused on asking two core questions:

- What does it take to be an effective leader?
- What can the rest of us learn, even if we work in a completely different industry or discipline?

Each leader I interviewed considered how their approach to managing others changed and evolved over time. This included their reactions, motivations and the outcomes they achieved. Through looking deeply within themselves and their organisations, these leaders confronted ethical dilemmas, areas of avoidance, the unsaid and sometimes even the unsayable.

To these responses I have offered beneath the surface or psychoanalytic interpretations, developed through working and coaching leaders across more than 35 different nationalities, cultures and organisational systems.

I believe looking beneath the surface generates more depth, daring and intensity of insight. I believe it gives leaders more emotional bandwidth and inner resources to cope with the relentless pressures many of them face in the course of their work. It should be noted though that a psychoanalytic approach risks generating interpretations or hypotheses that may be ingenious and creative, but wrong. It is important therefore not to regard such ideas as absolutes, but rather to consider them with a light touch and to be open to letting go of a hypothesis, in order to generate better alternatives.

Why this book matters

Performance flourishes when people enjoy their work. Investing in the quality of a conversation, the quality of our presence and the quality of our listening are important leadership decisions with as much potential to influence outcomes and success as knowing which stock to buy or what to let go of.

Emerging alongside the writing of this book, is a call for higher ethics in leadership. This is about inward honesty and outward consistency. It includes revealing bad practice and amplifying good leadership. We need greater diversity of thinking to deliver healthy, sustainable and sustaining organisations.

My appeal for higher ethics in leadership resonates with the disruption being witnessed in almost every field of employment. Despite it being (mostly but by no means always) illegal, to hire or fire people on the basis of age, colour, sexual preference or life stage, nor to inappropriately touch, pressurise or sexually assault colleagues or staff, evidence that this perpetuates continues to emerge. Perhaps its emergence is not about prevalence, but about it becoming safe to voice what has been going on. This is the era of being believed.

There are plenty of business models and academic papers on leadership and organisational design. However this book has offered contemporary, in-depth thinking. It is a learning resource for today's leaders and future leaders. It offers the reader a vehicle in which to stimulate and reflect upon their personal and professional growth. Also, to improve the thinking, shaping and eventual sustainability of the companies and organisations which make up the working world and our society as a whole.

I believe leading with higher ethics and integrity has the potential to increase productivity, profit, sustainability and joy in coming to work.

May each of us identify where – be it at home, at work or in the community – our individual gifts and insights are needed most.

Index